THE
Miracle
OF
Prayer

Also by Pat Boone

TWIXT TWELVE AND TWENTY
A NEW SONG
A MIRACLE A DAY KEEPS THE DEVIL AWAY
GET YOUR LIFE TOGETHER
BETWEEN YOU, ME, AND THE GATEPOST
THE CARE AND FEEDING OF PARENTS
THE REAL CHRISTMAS
JOY
DR. BALAAM'S TALKING MULE
THE HONEYMOON'S OVER (with Shirley Boone)

The Miracle of Prayer

Pat Boone

Zondervan Books
Zondervan Publishing House
Grand Rapids, Michigan

THE MIRACLE OF PRAYER
Copyright © 1980 by Pat Boone

Zondervan Books are published by the
Zondervan Publishing House
1415 Lake Drive, S.E., Grand Rapids, Michigan 49506

Library of Congress Cataloging-in-Publication Data

Boone, Pat.
   [Pray to win]
   The miracle of prayer / by Pat Boone.
      p.   cm.
   Reprint. Originally published: Pray to win. New York :
Putnam, © 1980
   ISBN 0-310-22131-5
   1. Prayer. 2. Success—Religious aspects—Christianity.
I. Title.
   [BV210.2.B645 1989]
   248.3'2—dc19   88-33701
                                            CIP

Printed in the United States of America

89 90 91 92 93 94 / AK / 10 9 8 7 6 5 4 3 2 1

PROFOUND THANKS TO BILL PROCTOR for wading through the complexity of my schedule and helping me to get my thoughts in order and this book on paper. We've both learned a lot more about praying and winning as we worked together.

This effort is gratefully dedicated to all those folks who've opened my eyes to the limitless triumphs available through prayer.

CONTENTS

Part I How to Start a Supernatural Conversation

1. Language Without Limits: An Introduction to Prayer Power   11
2. Prayer Probes   19
3. The Action-Prayer Principle   34

Part II The Winning Prayer Formula

4. The Fiddler Factor   43
5. The Practical Side of Private Prayer   54
6. Prerequisites for Prayer Power   66
7. Battle of Wits, Wisdom and Will   86
8. The Multiple Effect   99
9. Choosing Your Prayer Frequency   109
10. How to Listen for Supernatural Answers   124

11. God's Special Communication Codes   142

Part III Exploring the Frontiers
of Prayer Power

12. The Language of Love Is Learned at Home 161
13. The Prayer Prescription   173
14. The Root of All Riches   194
15. How to Mix Prayer and Politics   206
16. Can You Talk Your Way Into the
      Winner's Circle?   219
      Conclusion:
      Final Thoughts on Winning Big   233

PART I
How to Start a Supernatural Conversation

1 Language Without Limits: An Introduction to Prayer Power

Speech doesn't exist.
You have never uttered an intelligible word, nor heard one.

Try, just for a moment, to wipe all language out of your mind. It will require a very fertile imagination and an exercise of will to do it, but I hope you'll try. Imagine a world that has never known the spoken word.

If you're anything like me, you quickly begin to see that human history would have to be drastically different. All the way back to Adam, man's activities would have to be juggled and rearranged, and a great deal of what we call progress would have to be scrapped. Just try to conceive of people carrying on daily tasks, or people joking and laughing with one another about *anything*, or more importantly, trying to establish deep, meaningful personal relationships.

Man is resourceful, so he would surely have come up

with some way to accomplish these things—but it would be infinitely harder, and therefore slower. Most likely, personal relationships would suffer the most, without the nuances, the shadings, and the infinite variety of spoken words.

Of course, there are people with physical limitations who are unable to speak, and they often engage in loving relationships with others. I wonder, though, if that would be possible without the comforting support of those who *can* provide information, wisdom and love through the spoken word? Without our everyday language, we surely would be able to convey something of what we're thinking through gestures, touch, facial expression or some other body language. But *talking* is the key channel that helps us break through to new plateaus in understanding one another.

Without this ability to communicate orally, we'd be stripped of one of the essential characteristics that makes us distinctive as human beings.

If what I'm saying makes sense, if you agree with me, nod your head. Better yet, go ahead and say "Yes" right out loud. Dramatize my point for me! Be grateful for language in a fresh new way, grateful for this God-given ability to communicate ideas and feelings, directions and discoveries with other people. We take it for granted much too much.

Perhaps I should backtrack just a moment. I used the phrase "God-given"; do you grant me that? Do you agree with me that the special characteristics and abilities that elevate us above purely animal life are somehow transferred to us through some operation of a benevolent creator? If you don't, we may have some difficulty really communicating through this book, because I believe fundamentally that we have the process and miracle of speech for two basic reasons: to communicate with each other and to communicate with God Himself. Now, even if you don't agree with me on that point right away, I hope you'll at least accept that as a vital premise for our ongoing discussion, because *praying to win* is obviously a futile activity if there is no God to pray to, and no God to answer our prayers and work with us toward the accomplishing of our objectives.

So, at least for the purpose of our discussion, let's agree that there is a God, and that he's not only the Giver of speech—He means to be one of the prime *objects* of speech. I believe that's unquestionably the truth. And now put yourself in His place for just a moment. Or, in a simpler context, imagine yourself a parent whose child never speaks to you. You've done a great many good things for the child, you love that child enough to die for him or her, and you feel that the child is at least vaguely aware of your existence—but he or she never speaks to you at all! Wouldn't that distress you, displease you, perhaps even grieve you? Most likely, you'd try to communicate in some other way with that child, perhaps even physically or unpleasantly, if your need to communicate became strong enough. Dwell on that situation for a moment, and we'll move on.

Though spoken words are so vital in every other area of our lives, it's amazing to me that so many people neglect an area of interpersonal communication so important to personal and social growth as prayer. I almost hesitate to use the word, because most people, even among those who really *believe* in the existence of God, don't pray much at all, and a surprising percentage don't even feel they know how. And yet they talk incessantly! Though prayer does have its supernatural aspects, I really believe that the technique is as simple as discussion with another human being, with the head tilted slightly upward.

Clement of Alexandria once referred to prayer as "conversation with God," and I think he nailed it! That's probably the best definition you'll ever come across.

We humans have learned a great deal about how to influence and manipulate others through the spoken word. But even though many spiritual resources are available to us, we know woefully little about projecting our oral communications into the supernatural realm. When the word "prayer" is mentioned these days, notions of magic, superstition and ignorance frequently pop into mind. I've often encountered thinly masked amusement or a somewhat disconcerted and uncomfortable "Well, that's nice . . ." and a quick change of the subject.

And if a person starts talking about *dramatic answers* to prayer—especially "praying to win" in the sense of requesting God to respond with money, power, fame or some first-place finish in competition—the reaction may be an outright guffaw. A misunderstanding of what prayer is and how it's done can certainly result in silly, simplistic attempts to "get God to do something" for you, and these attempts *may* warrant a laugh or two. But I'm telling you—and I'll amply prove it—that the power of genuine prayer can result in incredible, miraculous happenings that can only be explained in supernatural terms. Here are a few examples of what I'm talking about.

—One man, who was on the verge of bankruptcy in an unprofitable business venture, needed $1.3 million immediately to pay off his creditors. Despairing, but still hopeful that God might be able to pull him out of this financial mess, he contacted two friends who prayed with him for a miracle. Within three days a buyer appeared and bought the ailing business for $2 million— more than enough to cover the outstanding debts!

—A young woman with a degenerative bone disease, which made it painful for her even to walk and for which she was told there was no cure, prayed that God would heal her. Almost immediately her legs were strengthened and her doctor called off a planned operation. She was soon out playing tennis with her friends.

—Two American tennis stars prayed for strength before a crucial Davis Cup Challenge Round, and they led their team to a close victory the next day to return the cup to the United States.

—A New Yorker who was short on money was returning from a visit to a sick friend in a hospital when he sensed God saying to him, "If you want money for a vacation this year, ask Me and you'll receive it." He did ask, and within three days he unexpectedly came by enough money to finance a trip with his wife to Bermuda.

—An evangelist without funds believed he should build a major university, so he prayed about it, and within a few years millions had become available to him to establish a major educational institution in the Southwest.

—A penniless law school graduate asked God for guidance in his life, and he felt God directing him to establish a Christian television network. Within a few years he was in charge of a huge international television and communications complex.

—A scientific researcher has reported that when group prayers are directed toward plants, even at a distance of several hundred miles, they grow faster than plants without the advantage of prayer.

—A multimillionaire broke his ankle by falling off a golf cart. The bone wouldn't heal properly, and X rays showed a wide separation remained in the bone. As a result, the doctor recommended an operation to insert a steel pin. The businessman refused and went to a prayer meeting, where the congregation prayed over his injury, and the next day his leg had healed completely.

—A businessman was flying on a plane which developed faulty landing gear. The passengers were told to brace for a crash landing, but the businessman visualized the landing mechanism and asked God to remedy the problem. The landing gear came right down and the relieved pilot executed a safe landing.

—A young entertainer who was completely broke went into a church and told God he would build an altar for Him if He would help him over this financial crisis. The entertainer became a famous comedian and, true to his word, he erected a hospital to fulfill his promise.

—A young skeptic who couldn't understand how anyone could really believe there is a God, nevertheless prayed, "If you're there, God, reveal yourself!" One night, as a result of these supplications, he felt his thoughts and emotions being taken over by a Force outside himself, and suddenly he had the conviction and faith that had always escaped him.

Have I whetted your interest?

Some of these things may not interest you at all, but I'll bet some of them do. You may not have any of these problems—but you've got *some* kind of need, some kind of problem, and I just want you to understand that approaching an interested and loving Creator/God can be your best option, not your last resort.

Each of these events has been reported and verified independently; they're not just "old wives' tales" or rumors. I'll go into exciting incidents like these in great detail in the pages ahead. The important thing to understand at this point is that there is a largely untapped power in the universe, a line of communication to a supernatural realm that most of us know far too little about. I've been studying, experimenting and immersing myself in the vocabulary and rhetoric of this supernatural language for a number of years, and I can identify wholeheartedly with the words of Tennyson in his *Morte d'Arthur:*

> More things are wrought by prayer
> Than this world dreams of. Wherefore, let thy voice
> Rise like a fountain for me night and day.

Some of the healings and financial windfalls mentioned above may seem so fantastic that they verge on the bizarre. But I've seen enough strange, miraculous things occur after intense prayer sessions to know that *anything can happen* when a group, whose members know the basic rules of effective divine communication, gather to offer up their requests.

What I want to explore in this book are the practical techniques you can employ to project your thoughts and wishes from the purely human plane into that spiritual dimension that is the source of extraordinary, superhuman events. "Winning" prayer is prayer which brings results—and your spiritual communications can be winners, if you just know how to speak the right language.

I believe it's quite possible to achieve success in any field by employing the right approach to prayer. Winning in life means living a healthy, happy existence in which you find fulfillment by striving toward and achieving your significant long-term goals.

No less an expert than Jesus of Nazareth said, in Mark 11:24, Revised Standard Version, ". . . I tell you, whatever you ask in prayer, believe that you receive it, and you will." I have personally found this statement to be literally true.

I don't mean that you can start playing the role of the greedy little child in a candy store and point to anything you vaguely think you might want and expect to receive it. Prayer doesn't work like that because God is too personal a Being to be interested in such an exploitative relationship with mankind. But God *does* want us to be contented and materially successful—and the right approach to prayer can guarantee this result.

Don't you like the sound of that word? I said *"guarantee!"*

The reason that most people come up losers in prayer is that they go about it in a haphazard, shoot-from-the-hip manner. If you're really interested in getting to know another individual, you make a commitment to spend a considerable amount of "quality" time in that other person's presence—and you try to make your conversations count. Or if you want to make a good impression and have the best chance of moving ahead in your job, you set goals, draw up a game plan and work at it until you succeed. Prayer requires much the same concentration and effort—but believe me, the possible goal achievements are far more impressive and rewarding.

If I sound crass or materialistic, I'm sorry. But there *are* material benefits in prayer, and far, far more. Stay with me.

The first step in becoming a powerful and fluent spokesman in this supernatural language I've been describing is to understand precisely what constitutes prayer and what means you can use to effectively propel your requests into the supernatural realm. These "prayer probes," as I call them—these words and phrases which are launched in such a way that they are heard and acted upon by God—are the next subject for us to consider.

2 Prayer Probes

If you want to learn how to pray effectively, go sit quietly in the country for a few hours, outside the clanging noise of civilization. Without any of the usual urban distractions, try listening to the voices of the woods and waters and animals around you.

A lily pad stirs on a ripple in a pond . . . the leaves in the trees rustle in a gentle breeze . . . a frog croaks . . . a mountain stream gurgles and dances in the morning sun . . . the surf from the ocean crashes on the rocks below you . . . one squirrel scurries after another in the underbrush . . . millions of miles away, a galaxy twinkles as one star.

Now, you might first think, "That's nothing—those are just the usual sounds and sights of nature!" But before you jump to any quick conclusions, you might also thumb through the Psalms and see what David and the other Old Testament poets say about these noises you're hearing. For example, take a look at Psalm

96:11–13, RSV: "Let the heavens be glad, and let the earth rejoice; let the sea roar, and all that fills it; *let the field exult, and everything in it!* Then shall all the trees of the wood sing for joy before the Lord, for he comes, for he comes to judge the earth. He will judge the world with righteousness, and the peoples with his truth."

What I'm getting at is this: perhaps this natural activity you're witnessing has a purpose. Perhaps this is not just some random, cacophonous rustling and bubbling. Instead, the sounds and sights before you may be part of the natural groaning and creaking and "tuning" that a giant orchestra must go through before the various individual instruments can be gathered together into one powerful, melodious symphonic sound. Or, as one hymn writer has put it, ". . . all nature sings and round us rings the music of the spheres."

These individual cries and movements in the natural world have always seemed to me to be part of the universal communication between the Creator and His creation—in just the way that the cooing and happy gurgling of a little baby sparks joy in the heart of its proud parent. The world in general is in bad shape now—primarily because of the terrible things that men and women have done to themselves and to the earth. But occasionally, the song of an individual bird or the soothing sound of a quiet brook will reach out and encompass you and, I believe, lift you into a spiritual sensitivity beyond the physical world. It's wonderful, and it's happened to me many times; I'm sure it has to you, but that is *not* the primary purpose of that noise, that bird-song, that babbling, or rustling, or frog-croak. No, the original intent of those happy songs is communication, a kind of conversation with fellow creatures and with their Creator.

A lot of the natural sound of nature is pure joy, spontaneous exultation, uninhibited praise for a Creator/God, for life itself! I don't mean that birds and animals *consciously* think of God and direct praise toward Him; instead, they are actually programmed with this ability and this need to express joy, to verbalize and demonstrate life, and God Himself harvests those sounds like a farmer his most treasured crop.

Sound far-fetched? I'll illustrate. I had a personal encounter with the communication of praise in the world of nature a few years ago when I was visiting my parents in Nashville. (I told this story in greater detail in *A Miracle a Day Keeps the Devil Away*, published by Fleming H. Revell). I was rocking back and forth by myself on our porch swing one evening in late summer. I'd eaten a great Mama-cooked dinner, and I was thinking back over the countless ways Mama and Daddy had provided a warm home life while I was growing up. The most important thing my parents had given me was a sense that God loves me, and as I thought about my past life in and around this old neighborhood, I started thanking God for how good He had been to me. Through marriage and career problems, through anxieties and pressures and tensions, and all kinds of complexities that only an entertainer can appreciate, God had provided me with spiritual resources and an inner stability that had been far too important in my life for me even to try to measure.

It all came into sharp focus that night on the porch swing.

I spent a long time telling Him how much I appreciated Him and recounting and pondering many of the things He had done for me. Then, still feeling a joyous gratitude, but having run out of ordinary words to express my feelings, I began to sing in a mysterious, supernatural language that had become a regular part of my prayer life. But more about that later—the important thing for now is that while this spontaneous melody and

21

fluent, but unknown, words came from my lips, I was suddenly enveloped by a harmonious burst of sound from the bushes around me.

At first it startled me, but after a moment I laughed— the crickets in the yard and plants around our house had joined me! They were doing exactly what *I* was doing! We were singing together in an uninhibited chorus of praise to God, thanking Him for creating our worlds and giving us life; actually, we were just agreeing with His own pronouncement about His creation in the Book of Genesis: "It is good"!

Now you may say, "Well, those crickets were going to start singing together anyhow; you didn't have anything to do with it." And you're probably right; crickets do have a way of singing together like that most every night. That's the natural part. The *super*natural part is the timing—I started my solo first, and then the chorus joined in! We made some beautiful music together and it was a spine-tingling experience for me. Right away, I thought of what the Psalmist said in Psalm 96:12, RSV: "Let the field exult, and everything in it!"

Perhaps you've felt your own heart skip a beat during a similar experience—when you witnessed just the right configuration of sun, sky, clouds and splashes of color in a sunset. And perhaps something deep inside you suggested, "This kind of beauty has to be more than just a coincidence. The convergence of this natural beauty and my inner response to it is doing something special to me. It makes me want to shout for joy!"

If you've been through such an event, you've experienced what I call a "prayer probe"—a brief but extremely poignant and personally significant encounter with the spiritual realm which surrounds us constantly, but which too often we neglect or ignore entirely, except during one of these involuntary, "breakthrough" experiences.

Prayer probes may also occur in other circumstances, however. For example, everyone has heard of the "foxhole prayer," where the soldier is flat on his stomach, with shells exploding nearby and bullets whining next to his ear. Many a frightened infantryman has muttered through chattering teeth, "Oh, God, if You'll just get me through this, I'll live for You from here on!" But often the probes are never "retrieved," in the sense that they never come back to have a lasting effect on that life. Like a deep-space probe, they may have a brief impact and send back some interesting and perhaps comforting information, but then they go "dead" and are forgotten.

That's not always the case, though. Sometimes a "foxhole" prayer really *changes* things! Clint Walker, for example, tells about the time when he took a fall on the snow as he was skiing downhill at top speed. As he tumbled through the snow, *his ski pole penetrated his heart.* Utterly alone and apparently dying in the frozen silence, he cried, "God, I'm really in trouble! I can't help myself. I'm not going to make it unless You see me through—and I *would* like to stay around awhile. . . ."

Rescuers arrived soon afterward and whisked him off to a hospital, where fast, effective surgery saved his life. Soon after, he was telling the world about it on television. And he'll tell you today that his life has changed.

In my travels around the country, I'm constantly running into equally dramatic instances of answered prayers—even though the person doing the praying may not be committed to any particular spiritual viewpoint. For example, a Canadian woman I know, who is Jewish, though not particularly religious, was in a Catholic hospital, suffering from a stroke. As she lay there in a semiparalyzed state, feeling tremendously afraid because she didn't know whether she was going to live or die, her eyes focused on a wooden cross hanging on the wall. That religious symbol prompted her to cry out, "Help me!" Her anguished, deeply felt prayer apparently got through, even though she really didn't know to whom or what she was praying—because she made quite an amazing overnight comeback and was soon released from the hospital!

But one of the most dramatic examples I've encountered of how a series of sincere prayer probes can change a person's life, both physically and spiritually, involved a young man in his early twenties named Bill Dooner. Bill was an alcoholic who spent much of his time on the Bowery in New York City, drinking and sleeping in doorways and selling his blood to hospitals to get enough money for his next drink. Aware of the hopelessness of his situation, he found himself reaching out for Something beyond himself.

"I guess that in some ways, praying is taking your thoughts and lifting them up," he said. "I would be on the end of a bar on Third Avenue, and I would envision things. At the times when my head wasn't in the toilet, throwing up, I would have these illusions, or dreams. And there were five or six things that constantly reappeared in this dream pattern. The first was to be released from my addiction to alcohol, to be able to lift a glass of ginger ale, without having it drive me crazy. Another one was not to live in the city anymore, but to live in a suburban community. One was to hit a modicum of wealth, of independence, because wealth spelled freedom for me. Another one was that I would be in the field of advertising and selling, because those were the areas I had stumbled into—and been fired from, time after time. And finally, one was to marry a real fine girl and have real nice children.

"And do you know—every one of those things has come true! I can tell you there was no way that somebody with that kind of track record, with his head on the bar, was going to have those things come true without God."

Bill Dooner is now a multimillionaire who owns a number of thriving businesses, including billboard advertising companies and motel and restaurant chains. But it took a number of years—about twenty, in fact—for God to answer all those flash prayers that were sent out from those New York bars. First of all, Bill fell in with a group of reformed alcoholics and was able to overcome his drinking problems. His freedom from alcohol enabled him to release his money-making talents and realize his dreams of a successful business career. Finally, he met and fell in love with Ellie, a Mennonite girl who became the wife he had always hoped for—and they soon found themselves the proud parents of five healthy, bright children.

All of Bill's dreams had been realized and his prayer probes had brought forth more than enough fruit—or so it seemed. Actually, something was still missing from his and Ellie's lives, and Ellie was the first to recognize that "crisis prayers" weren't enough to satisfy. She wanted a deeper experience, one which would allow her to move beyond those quick prayer probes to a more meaningful, conversational relationship with God. This inner yearning finally overwhelmed her one evening while she was at home alone. She didn't know where to turn for help, so she just collapsed on her bed and cried, "God, if You're really there, You've got to open some doors, so we can walk in."

It was yet another prayer probe from the Dooner family—but this time more intense than anything that had come before. And that very night, when Ellie went to the grocery store, she ran into a friend who said, "Ellie, I've been thinking about you." This woman invited her to a meeting some Christians were holding the next Friday night, and Ellie quickly accepted. There was no doubt in her mind that God was in the process of answering her prayer, and she was eager to see exactly what He had in mind.

Ellie soon became a regular at this Christian group, and she came back with stories of healings and other answered prayers that fascinated her children—but made Bill feel very uncomfortable and even hostile. "Listen, she's nuts sometimes, and you have to be patient with her," Bill told the kids. "When she comes down, she'll be more realistic, but until then I don't want you guys to listen to her."

But then an agonizing personal crisis struck Bill. He was injured when a golf cart overturned and left him with a fractured ankle and a badly lacerated arm. Doctors in Jefferson City, Missouri, near the spot where the accident had occurred, put a cast on his leg, and he had every reason to expect that his leg would be as good as new in a few weeks. For some reason, however, the ankle failed to mend properly. The cast was removed and replaced in Knoxville, Tennessee, where he maintained an apartment when he was in the South on business. The rest of the family was living in Ireland at that time, in a mansion once occupied briefly by Jacqueline Kennedy Onassis, and Bill commuted regularly across the Atlantic to be with them.

When it was time for the second cast to be removed six weeks later, he had the job done in Waterford, Ireland, but the ankle was still painful. The Irish doctor fitted Bill with a short walking cast, but it was impossible for him to get around without pain. The pain got so bad that he actually had to go to an emergency room at Northwestern Memorial Hospital in Chicago while he was there on business. The doctor there took an X ray, and as Bill recalled, the physician "showed me the picture, and there was a wide separation in the bone, maybe an eighth of an inch." This doctor wanted to admit him for immediate surgery to put a steel pin in the broken bone, but Bill refused because he wanted to get right back to Knoxville. The orthopedist reluctantly gave him a new cast and a pair of crutches and sent him on his way with a warning to see a doctor in Knoxville without delay.

Despite his pressing business schedule, Bill Dooner did follow the Chicago doctor's advice and made an appointment with the best orthopedist he could find in Knoxville. But before he went for the examination, he decided that maybe it wouldn't hurt to try to invoke a little supernatural aid. So he got in touch with a friend of his who worked with a Christian organization in town, and the man told Bill where he might find a local prayer meeting.

The millionaire attended the prayer session, and when the leader asked if anyone had a prayer request, Bill described his problem and asked them to pray for him. "They asked me if I wanted to go up to the front of the room, and I said no, I'd just stay where I was. And so they just prayed over me." It wasn't until the next day, back in the apartment, that he felt the results of that prayer: "All of a sudden there was this sharp pain, so sharp that I cried out," he said. "And then, nothing." A couple of days later, he went to the doctor as scheduled, even though the pain in his ankle had disappeared mysteriously. The physician did a thorough examination, and his findings are recorded in this report:

TO WHOM IT MAY CONCERN:

This will certify the above captioned (William Dooner) was examined by me on Oct. 9, 1975, with a long history of difficulty in his left ankle, dating back to July 12, when he fell out of a golf cart and injured his ankle.

He was seen at that time by an orthopedist who told him he had a fracture of what sounds like the distal fibula, and he was casted.

The cast was removed and he was told he had in addition a fracture of the inside of the ankle, and from his description it sounds like the medial malleolus; he was placed in another cast at that time. This man is quite busy in his occupation; he travels all over the world, including Ireland and Chicago, and he has been seen on at least one occasion in each location, and on his last visit to an emergency room in Chicago, he was told he might have to have surgery. He was seen by me for a definitive opinion about his ankle.

Examination revealed the patient to be in a short leg cast. This was removed and on examination range of motion was good, there was no tenderness over the medial side of the ankle and virtually no swelling in the ankle. There was no tenderness over the fibula and he had no instability. X rays of the left ankle revealed a healed, or healing, fracture of the medial malleolus in good position; it was undisplaced. I could not readily identify a fracture of the fibula at the time of this examination.

He was advised since three months had elapsed since the time of his injury I felt he could certainly be out of the cast and he was sent to physical therapy for exercises including heel cord stretching, and it was suggested he bear weight to tolerance.

In other words, Bill Dooner's badly broken ankle had healed in a matter of a few days, if not instantaneously, after that prayer meeting.

For an intelligent fellow like Dooner, the dramatic results of his latest attempt at prayer made it clear to him that he would be foolish not to learn more about this supernatural language and the Supreme Being who was the source of it. Periodic prayer probes had led to miraculous happenings just in themselves, but what might happen if he really made a commitment to God and wholeheartedly applied himself to becoming fluent in this extranormal form of communication?

Besides, he had other problems that he was having trouble resolving by himself. Even though there was plenty of money—more every day, in fact—Bill felt a hollowness inside him, a hollowness that even these amazing prayers couldn't fill. He needed something else, but he still wasn't sure exactly what. Then, one day, as he drove along an interstate highway, he recalled something that Ellie had said: "If you have a problem, take it and turn it over to the Holy Spirit."

He stopped the car right then and prayed: "I prayed to God the Father, and I prayed to Jesus, and I asked the Holy Spirit to come into my heart, my head, my stomach, my liver, my arms and legs, every part of me," he said. "All of a sudden, it was like an air bag had filled up the car—the Spirit just filled me up. And I cried, and thanked God for saving me. And for the rest of the drive, I don't think the tires were even touching the road."

Bill Dooner had decided *to move beyond those tentative, exploratory prayers that had been so beneficial to him and establish a deep, personal relationship with the very Source of prayer.*

That old Bible on the shelf, of course, is replete with similar cases of those who first tried a few tentative encounters with God and then decided that maybe He would be a good person to get to know better. And they immediately began to explore the more sophisticated facets of divine communication. One of the most striking examples of a man who persisted in sending out prayer probes was the Roman centurion Cornelius, who was stationed with the Italian Cohort at the port city of Caesarea. (See Acts 10) The Bible says that he was "a devout man who feared God": he probably had been drawn to worship the Hebrew God in some fashion without actually converting to Judaism. He also gave alms liberally and "prayed constantly to God"; and after a considerable amount of such persistence, he had a vision of an angel who said, "Your prayers and your alms have ascended as a memorial before God." The angel told him to send messengers to the Apostle Peter, a Jew, who was residing just to the south in Joppa. Cornelius obeyed, and within hours, through the reluctant ministry of Peter, he and his family were ushered into an explosive new dimension of prayer and life. It's one of the most exciting stories in the old black Book!

The problem with most of us is that after we've sent out those prayer probes, we don't take time to *listen* as closely as Cornelius did. If he had failed to sit quietly and devote a significant amount of time to prayer, his visions of the angel might never have occurred. The evidence for God is all around us, and He frequently tries to break through our overbearing self-centeredness and egotism to begin a dialogue with us; but we are simply too busy to listen.

I recall one interchange on television between talk show host Merv Griffin and evangelist Oral Roberts. Merv, really putting Oral on the spot, asked, "I hear that you've actually heard God speak to you—is that right?"

Oral waited a second or two; then he eyed Merv with a slight smile and responded, "Merv, God's spoken to *you* many times, too—haven't you heard Him?"

Merv immediately went to a commercial, so I don't know what was going through his mind, but I think Oral had a good point. *God speaks to each one of us,* and He loves us.

Are you aware of this in your own life?

Have you heard God speaking to you, probing into your own heart and life at any time? You'll be a very rare individual if you haven't. Almost every human being has at one time or another in his life felt a distinct sense of the presence and existence of a Creator/God, and a longing to develop some kind of communication.

But we tend to draw back before that communication becomes very intimate or real. I suppose we're just a little frightened, aren't we? C. S. Lewis compares it to a little boy with a string tied to some imaginary creature in a dark closet; the boy playfully tugs at the string and imagines that he is pulling some beast out of the mounds of clothes and shoes and paraphernalia—when suddenly he thinks he feels a resisting and opposite tug on the other end! His heart begins to pound, his eyes widen and he may drop the string and run!

God Himself, in His own Bible, says that "it is a fearful thing to fall into the hands of the living God."

But consider the alternative.

What kind of destiny can you look forward to, can any of us look forward to, apart from His active participation in our lives? I am convinced that the "fearful" aspect of the relationship comes from lack of knowledge, the factor of the unknown, and that increased involvement and productive communication begins to wipe all the fear away. And so, prayer probes are extremely useful, in that they establish a beginning contact with a God who is on the other end of the line, also probing into our lives and eager (more than we can imagine) to *develop* a two-way communication.

It's the same situation that any father finds himself in when his infant begins to reach out to him, begins to recognize him, to laugh with delight when he sees his father's face—the reaching out of those little, stubby, dimpled hands is absolutely irresistible to the proud father! The baby's attempt at communication may be limited and inadequate, but the father is delighted with the attempt and will work with this child to develop and broaden the possibilities of their communication and their ongoing relationship.

God is just like that.

Unfortunately, foxhole prayers, crisis-oriented prayer probes, last-ditch efforts to get some kind of divine help when everything else has failed, are simply not enough in themselves. Even when they bring miraculous results, if that's all that happens, it won't really matter very much in the long run. In the movie *The End*, Burt Reynolds swims far out to sea, intending to drown himself because he's heard he has a fatal disease. But once he's out way too far, he becomes frightened and begins to pray fervently, promising God that he'll be a good, deeply religious person if he can just make it back to shore. And so, he turns and swims toward home. But the closer to shore that he gets, the less fervent his prayers become. Finally—when he steps out on dry land—he's completely forgotten his frightened prayers and is prepared to live the same roguish life he was living before. The audience, of course, is in stitches by the end of the scene, and it *is* quite funny. But the humor has a serious edge, because the behavior of Burt's character is precisely the way most of us try to relate to God. We'd like to maintain a hotline to heaven—for emergencies only.

It's not likely to work that way.

Prayer probes are important, they're vital, but they should be just the beginning and not the end. It's important to recognize that God *wants* to communicate with you as much as with anyone else—no matter how bad a person you may think you are. *And no prior knowledge or theological training is required.* You can just say, "Look, God, I really don't know anything about the Bible, or Christianity, or Judaism, or Jesus or anything. In fact, I'm not even sure if You're out there—for all I know, I may be talking to myself. But if You *are* out there, please show me something about Yourself—be real to me in some way that I can recognize."

Just be honest! God knows what you're thinking, so

there's no sense in beating around the bush with Him. Tell Him exactly what you're thinking, and believe me, He'll honor your candor.

You don't have to learn some special prayer jargon to start a conversation with God. Honesty and a willingness to establish a personal relationship with Him are the only initial requirements. God is looking for an opportunity to reveal Himself to you, so if you put Him to the test and then watch for an answer without too many preconceptions about how that answer will come, *I can guarantee you* that you'll be in for some exciting surprises.

So go ahead. If you haven't done it before, or even if you have, fire off a probe of some kind, whether it's a quiet, tentative sentence or two, expressing a need or concern; whether it's just a phrase or two about how you'd like to establish some sort of relationship with a Creator/God, if He's there someplace; or whether it's an honest and desperate cry for help—go ahead, and do it in your own words, in your own way. I promise that prayer will not fall on deaf ears, and that you *will* receive a response, probably in some unmistakable and dramatic way. But when it happens, don't consider that that's an end in itself—it's only the beginning!

There *is* a tugging at the other end of the line—but don't run away!

3 The Action-Prayer Principle

There is an old Russian proverb which advises, "Pray to God, but row for the shore."

There's also the story of the Catholic priest who answered, when he was asked which of two praying boxers God might bless in the ring, "Probably the better puncher!"

There's truth as well as humor here. An initial prayer probe or two may bring wonderful results, and they can be a great way to begin communication with God; but a person who wants to learn truly winning prayer will have to move beyond that stage to what I call the "action-prayer principle." This principle, simply put: *whenever we pray, we must at the same time be willing, if necessary, to be an instrument for the answering of that prayer.*

You've heard, "God helps those who help themselves"—and I believe that's true. But I doubt that you could stretch that axiom to include Al Capone or Adolf Hitler or Idi Amin, so it's clearly not a universal precept. There must be qualifications there somewhere. I'm not talking about a "do it yourself plan," but I do believe that a *willingness* to be involved in the answer to a prayer is a vital prerequisite to success.

I constantly bump into two common approaches to prayer, and neither gives God much of a chance to demonstrate His power. On the one hand, some people feel that they have to do everything themselves (after asking God's blessings) and that it's not a good idea to leave anything in the hands of a Supreme Being. At the other extreme, there are those who toss out a prayer from their armchairs and sit back waiting for an answer, without any thought that perhaps they could get into the act to help bring about those things which they've asked for. Both approaches may be doomed to failure. God certainly wants you to test Him and give Him a chance to do great things for you; but you can't always just lie down, shake a tree and expect all the best fruit to drop into your lap; nor can you ask God to be your butler and bring your pipe and slippers.

Effective prayer is most often a combination of speaking the request and then *doing* what you can do to bring the desired blessing about. This principle seems to have been operative since the earliest Old Testament times. The Patriarch Abraham, for example, had gone without children until he and his wife, Sarah, were well past child-bearing age. But still he prayed, "O Lord God, what wilt thou give me, for I continue childless and the heir of my house is Eliezer of Damascus? . . . Behold, thou has given me no offspring; and a slave born in my house will be my heir." (Genesis 15:2–3, RSV)

God responded, "This man shall not be your heir; *your own son shall be your heir.*" But Abraham was not allowed to lie back in the hammock and wait for the cries of a baby son. Mull this over: before he even got down to the obvious necessity, and in his advanced age, the Lord demanded that he circumsize himself and all the males of his household!

Would you have done it?

Doesn't make much sense to the human intellect, does it? Still though, the old Patriarch complied, and sure enough, God gave him his son, Isaac—even though Abraham was one hundred years old and Sarah was ninety! A pretty dramatic demonstration of action-prayer.

Of course, the converse of this principle is also true: after the initial prayer probe, if you simply go on mouthing prayers without taking any necessary accompanying action, it's quite likely that you'll come up a loser rather than a winner in your prayer efforts.

May I give you a personal example in which I *didn't* take my own advice?

I was participating in a celebrity basketball tournament on CBS-TV. The tournament was organized around a number of three-man teams, consisting of two professional basketball players and one show business personality on each. I was teamed up with David Thompson of the Denver Nuggets and Dick Van Arsdale, who formerly played for Phoenix. Although we faced some tough opponents, like actor William DeVane and the ex-All-Pro Dave DeBusschere, we won in the early round and moved into the semifinals against Kevin Dobson of the *Kojak* show, George McGinnis of the Philadelphia 76ers, and a pro player-coach, Kevin Loughery.

I wanted to win, because my team had lost in the finals the previous year and because I was the oldest man in the whole contest—and I wasn't sure I'd have any more chances. When I pray to win in an athletic event, I'm always willing for the Lord to overrule me, because He's involved with a lot of other folks there too, but if it can go either way, I want my bid in early. And win or lose, I really wanted to do my best and make a good showing, and I felt I'd be able to help my pro teammates if I shot more often—especially from outside the twenty-five-foot line, because celebrities who scored from that distance could get three points instead of two for a basket. I'm usually a good long shot, so that was my strategy.

But when I got in the actual game, the pressure of the competition and the TV cameras caused me to forget the game plan that I had chosen after prayer. I took only two shots—one of them bounced off the rim and the other got blocked down my throat by Loughery, who knocked me down in the process. As it happened, my two teammates were guarded quite well by the other players, so it was very difficult to get passes into them and neither of them had a hot hand either. Big George McGinnis literally took control of the game, and his team beat us by three or four points.

It may seem silly for a grown man to get so concerned about the outcome of an amateur basketball game. But who likes to lose, anywhere or anytime? And on national television? Besides, I not only wanted to win for my sake, but for the sake of the two pros who stood to make some real money, and who don't like to lose, either. They may have been embarrassed enough at having to play basketball with a middle-aged grandfather!

But the worst part about this episode was that I had *prayed* about this game ahead of time, and had a definite sense of what I should do to cooperate with my own prayer—and then I didn't do it! I really never gave the Lord an adequate chance to bless me and help me make a real contribution. I kept trying to feed the ball to my well-guarded partners instead of taking the shots I knew I was qualified to take—and we lost the game. I'm not saying we would have *won* if I'd taken more shots, but then again we might have.

Later, sitting alone in my room and pouting, a picture of David and Goliath flashed into my mind. I saw David stepping forward to challenge Goliath (and right then Goliath looked exactly like George McGinnis). David didn't hesitate to get that stone flying from his sling, and God blessed him in that battle and helped him to become King of Israel. I suddenly felt certain that if David had missed with that first shot, he would have loaded up and shot again and wouldn't have quit until he or Goliath was dead. And I supposed if he had been in this basketball game, he would probably have kept tossing those balls up at the rim until some went in.

I could almost hear the Lord telling me, "Look, you prayed to win, you asked to contribute—why didn't you load your sling and shoot?"

I've just returned from the Bonneville salt flats in Utah, where my dear friend Stan Barrett has just established a new land speed record, driving a rocket car across the salt flats at 638 miles an hour! It was a heart-stopping and death-defying event, and Stan didn't go into the challenge without prayer. In fact, Shirley and I met with Stan and his wife, Penny, just moments before he left the trailer to get into the car for the climactic run, and committed the whole thing to God, earnestly asking for His blessing and protection. But then, *Stan got in the car and drove like crazy, risking his life on God's answer to his prayer!* That's the stuff from which winning prayers are fashioned. It's an active partnership with a creator God.

Listen to Donald V. Seibert, the Chairman and Chief Executive Officer of the J. C. Penney Company. "My personal view is that *the Lord works through individuals,* for the most part," Seibert observes. "When I pray, I should pray on the basis that I'm willing to be the instrument He uses to answer that prayer. Or if I'm concerned about some problem, I should be willing to be the solution to that problem instead of just offering up some general prayer that I want that problem to be solved."

Although Seibert has reached the top rung on his chosen career ladder, he says he's never prayed specifically that he would get a certain promotion or beat out a competitor. "I just pray that I can do the best I can, that

I'll make the right decisions. But I can't remember ever praying for an advantage in any situation. I guess that while we have assurance that our prayers will be answered, we also know that they will be answered within the context of God's will or plan. I'm reminded of the parable that Jesus told of the nobleman who was about to take a trip to a far country. (Luke 19: 11–27) This man called ten of his servants together and gave each of them a gold coin and instructed them, 'Trade with these until I come.' When he returned, he looked with approval on one who had earned an additional coin and another who had turned his single coin into five more. But he was quite harsh on a third servant who had simply put aside his coin without trying to multiply it with intelligence and hard work.

"In other words, it seems to me that it's the guy who sits on his talents who has the problem. Even though two people may be uneven in abilities, they may both be doing God's will as long as each is doing his best. That's the way I try to frame my prayers. I ask to be the best participant that I'm able to be. Of course, when you pray to do your best, that burdens you with a personal responsibility of preparing yourself to the fullest extent that you can—doing your homework, getting all the facts, employing the best judgment that you can in making decisions."

One very practical way that Seibert combines prayer and action is the procedure he employs to get caught up when he returns from a lengthy business trip. "My desk might be like this with mail," he says, raising his hand several feet off it. "The phone is ringing off the hook and people are waiting in the hall to see me. You can get rattled in that kind of situation if you don't step back and realize who you are, and do things one at a time. And all this relates back to the inner peace that I get from prayer. Without the support of my own prayer life, I might start in on one pile of work and out of the corner of my eye I see another pile that needs an equal amount of work. It would be very easy never to get through with that first pile because I wouldn't be concentrating on it. But when I pray to God for help, things are different. I don't know, theologically, how it works all the time: often, those prayers are certainly a direct communication to God. But they also help me to get a sense of perspective on the situation. I'm able to say, 'Wait a minute! Why are you getting excited? You know how to do all these things and you can only do them one at a time, so let's get organized and do them!'"

I think it was Francis of Assisi who prayed, "Lord, *make me an instrument* of thy peace." God did—and eight hundred years later, we're still talking about it!

That's the point, then; I won't belabor it further. If you're really serious about reaching your goals, and you understand that prayer can play a very important part, you'll have to make a commitment. You can't stand off on the side and sort of dabble in prayer, and expect to get anyplace. Whether you fully perceive it or not, you've got a loving Father who wants to help you accomplish your objectives, but He's saying to you, "Okay, roll up your sleeves and let's get started!" He *may* do it without you—He certainly can if He wants to—but chances are, He'll expect you to do your part.

And don't be so quick to give up, either. If what you're after doesn't occur right away, hang in there. Be just as consistent as a fledgling salesman who's determined to capture that big account. You're developing a new *language*, after all, the most powerful means of communication there is—and even German, Japanese, French or Hebrew require energy and attention over a period of time if you want to gain fluency.

God certainly does help those who help themselves. Especially if they let Him lead.

PART II
The Winning Prayer Formula

4   The Fiddler Factor

Prayer can be so simple.

Mysterious, yes; profound, infinitely; but so easy to do it's almost embarrassing. It *is* embarrassing to many of us! If it were much harder, if it took some kind of college training, if it were even more expensive in some way, a lot more folks might pray.

But the childlike simplicity of prayer is one of its greatest strengths.

Remember Tevye in *Fiddler on the Roof*? I love the image of this unaffected, unpretentious Russian Jew who pushes his milkcart along and carries on a running dialogue with the Almighty. He knows words are not always necessary for him to get his message across, either. If something goes wrong, he might just glance up toward heaven with a look that says, "Why? What did I do to deserve this, God?" A shrug or sigh might be enough to launch a prayer probe and get an effective divine conversation started.

Tevye shows us that conversation with God, like conversation with people, implies *a personal relationship*—and the more intimate the personal tie, the deeper and more meaningful the conversation. But so often I've heard agnostic or nonreligious friends and acquaintances say, "I don't understand what you mean by 'a personal relationship with God.'" And yet those same people develop and maintain personal relationships with other *people*, some of whom they hardly know! What they're really saying, then, is, "I don't even know this God at all, so how can I talk to Him?" That's a good and honest question, so let's talk about it.

The God who spoke this whole creation into existence is a Spirit who is much closer to you than a friend or relative, across town or across the country, engaging you in a phone conversation. And He doesn't usually speak in an audible voice out of the clouds, or through a plastic earpiece. But to get this divine conversation in gear, you may have to rid yourself of certain misconceptions. For example, God never meant us to fragment or compartmentalize our lives in order to "get religion." Too many people, when they decide to get serious about their relationship with God, often for the sake of their families, decide that going to church on Saturday or Sunday will take care of it. They figure they'll dress up, take the wife and kids to a service, sing some songs and look pious, maybe even put a few bucks in the collection plate and then, when the religious day is finished, mutter inwardly, "Whew, now that I've got that behind me, I can go back to real life!"

Friend, that just won't get it—and I don't even think God likes it very much, if that's as far as it goes.

Did he mean for us to wear special clothes or to do all the peculiar things that we do on Saturdays or Sundays to signify that we're spiritual people? I heard one guy say the other day that he thought that church buildings—in fact the whole idea of going to church—was just ridiculous. "When we walk into a church," he said, "we often walk softly and take on this whole reverent approach to things, as if God resides exclusively at that church or synagogue and isn't in our bathroom or office. But if you believe that God is who He says He is in the Bible, that He's everywhere and nothing's hidden from Him, you ought to be whispering and reverent in your office and your bathroom just as you are at church—or you ought to forget that whispery, reverent stuff altogether."

I think he's right. Because God is everywhere, He's not asking for some unnatural behavior from us, especially not when we decide to sit down and have a heart-to-heart talk with Him.

Glance through the Old Testament, especially at David's words in the Psalms and at the Patriarchs' communications with God in the Pentateuch. These Hebrew men and women were so open and joyous and straightforward about their relationship with God that they apparently never considered limiting their conversation with Him to a building, tent or other special location. They approached Him in the mainstream of their lives, and He was right there. It worked, and it must have been exciting! I think we should do the same.

Either this relationship, this communication with God, is everyday and immediate— or it's stilted, inhibited and often meaningless. In his *Varieties of Religious Experience*, the great American philosopher William James defines prayer as "every kind of inward communication or conversation with the power recognized as divine." He goes on to say, "Prayer in this wide sense is the very soul and essence of religion."

On the subject of what a "personal relationship with God" really involves, James goes further:

"Religion is nothing if it be not the vital act by which

the entire mind seeks to save itself by clinging to the principle from which it draws its life. This act is prayer, by which term I understand no vain exercise of words, no mere repetition of sacred formulae, but the very movement of the soul, putting itself in a *personal relation of contact* with the mysterious power of which it feels the presence—it may be prayer even before it has a name by which to call it. Wherever this interior is lacking there is no religion; wherever, on the other hand, this prayer rises and stirs the soul, even in the absence of forms or doctrines, we have living religion."

In his view, this "personal relation of contact" with God does not involve some sort of passive, contemplative approach to life. No—it's active, vital, involved! As James puts it, "The fundamental religious point is that in prayer, spiritual energy, which otherwise would slumber, does become active, and spiritual work of some kind is effected really."

So you shouldn't be confused or put off by the term "personal relationship with God" or "personal relationship with Christ." In each of the three Biblical manifestations of God—the Father, the Son and the Holy Spirit—there is a personal quality which we can relate to in much the same way that we interact with another human being, yet with indescribably more depth, intimacy and power. When you first begin to talk seriously to God and move beyond that intermittent prayer-probe stage we discussed earlier, you may feel a little silly, as though you're talking to yourself or the thin air. I know. I've been there. But that sense of uncertainty or strangeness will soon pass as your talks with Him become more frequent and you develop a mental image of this Person that you're communicating with.

Some people I know have a strong sense that Jesus Himself is walking right there at their shoulder, listening and interacting with them throughout the day.

Others sense a warm, amorphous presence—perhaps the most appropriate image for the Holy Spirit, who is always ready to advise and guide them as they seek counsel. Of course, the particular image that you have of God is of little consequence so long as you approach Him and allow Him to approach you in a personal way. The late Christian writer and Cambridge don C. S. Lewis recognized in his *Letters to Malcolm: Chiefly on Prayer* that God is much more than a Person. But he still stressed that imagining God even in the most mundane terms—such as in the image of an old man on a throne in heaven—is better than not relating to him as a person at all. "What soul ever perished for believing that God the Father really has a beard?" Lewis asks.

Or look at it this way: if you had some business reason to call the Governor of Utah, and you'd never met the man, wouldn't you have a very favorable feeling toward him if he took your call personally and gave you every reason to believe that he would help you in accomplishing your purpose? Might you not look forward to the next call, and begin to form some kind of mental and visual impression of what he must look like; and would it matter very much if, when you met him in person, he didn't look like that at all?

Many people have also found that establishing a truly effective personal contact with God requires setting regular dates or appointments with Him. In other words, getting to know Him and learning to use the power of prayer may require that you be systematic. Other friendships don't flourish in an atmosphere of total neglect; well, it's much the same with God.

You may object, "I'm just not a disciplined enough person to set aside a regular time for prayer or devotionals each day! I work long hours and have too little time to spend with my family and friends as it is. How can I fit these prayer sessions into my schedule as well?"

I can sympathize with this viewpoint because I'm not as disciplined as I should be myself. I like to spend some time with the Lord first thing in the morning, but sometimes I sleep too late and another appointment comes pressing in and forces me to restrict or completely eliminate my devotional time. Or a family member may approach me early with some problem, and I'll have to deal with that.

But because my friendship with God is a real and living one, and because I have come to believe that I'm never out of His presence, I often start a conversation with Him before I even get out of bed. Usually, when I first open my eyes and realize that I'm awake, I'll just thank the Lord for a new day, for my health or for any other blessings that come to mind. Sometimes, I'll just say, "Good morning, Lord!" the very first thing. Right away, I'm aware of Someone on the other end of the line, and my perspective and priorities are set in order almost automatically. Speaking with Him from then on throughout the day seems natural and easy, as with any other friend.

Stay with me for a few more minutes in my normal morning, will you? After that initial "hello," I rarely jump up, grab a Bible and start reading. I'm a slow starter; it takes me about five or ten minutes just to make sure my blood is truly circulating and my eyes are likely to stay open for a while. I stir around a little bit, open the drapes to let some light in, slip into some jeans and make myself some lemon juice and water if I'm home. If I'm on the road, I settle for coffee. I almost always do some stretching exercises and a bunch of sit-ups, and by then I'm thoroughly awake.

Then I do my "spiritual breathing exercises."

This started some time back when I came across an

incredible statement by David in the 34th Psalm, RSV: "I will bless the Lord *at all times; His praise shall continually be in my mouth.*" I stopped and read that one again. It sounded nice, very spiritual—but how in the world could he do such a thing? David was a busy man, with a lot of talents and obligations; how could he be blessing the Lord at all times? Praise in his mouth continually? Later I came across Paul's admonition in 1 Thessalonians, 5:17, RSV, "pray constantly"! Again— how could such a thing be possible?

I thought about other things I do without ceasing, and prayer was certainly not one of them. My heart seems to beat consistently, and I breathe without ceasing—and that seemed to be about it. But wait! I remembered that, in the moment of man's creation, the Bible says that God lifted this freshly formed clay image of Himself to His own face, "breathed into his nostrils the *breath of life;* and man became a living being." (Genesis 2:7, RSV) That was man's original birth, and Adam was meant to be animated continually by that breath throughout eternity. But he blew it, according to the Bible, and his disobedience cut him off from God and doomed him to death. Jesus, the second Adam, *didn't* blow it, but remained faithful throughout his earthly life, animated by that same Holy breath, and made it possible for each of us to be born again, to be filled again with the very eternal breath of God. I had known that, basically, for years—but now it came into focus in a very intimate and practical way. I remembered that in the Bible, both the Old and New Testaments, the same Hebrew and Greek words are translated *spirit* or *breath.* The Hebrew *ruah* refers to the act of breathing out violently through the nose, and the word can also mean a very strong wind. The Greek *pneuma* means breath or Spirit, and they're used interchangeably in the New Testament.

So I decided to convert my breathing into "prayer

49

without ceasing!" and I often start first thing in the morning.

Quite simply, I raise my hands upward, visualizing my Heavenly Father and take a long, slow, deep breath. It feels wonderful, physically, but I'm literally asking the Lord to fill my lungs with His breath. I believe He does! As I exhale, I breathe His name, express thanks in simple ways, and often speak words of praise and endearment. I breathe this way a number of times, receiving His spirit/breath, and use the exhalation to voice my feelings toward Him. Sometimes I'll even ask for His forgiveness in certain specific areas, and it feels good to get the "dirty stuff" out of my system, along with the stale air. I don't have adequate words to tell you how much good this exercise does for me.

Does it sound nutty to you? Simplistic? Childish or just plain foolish? If so, I understand. But you have to be in my skin, to have tried the alternatives that I've tried, and *experience* the vitality and exhilaration that I have, in this primal, elemental exchange with a living Father/God. Don't knock it until you've tried it!

Now—most mornings, after my physical and spiritual exercises, I try to sit down and let Him speak directly to me out of His Word, the Bible. Even if I've only got five minutes, I'll usually turn to Proverbs, a thirty-one chapter gold mine of human and practical wisdom. It's a fantastic "how-to" book for practical living in this world. Then, I'll flip back into the book of Psalms, a hundred and fifty examples of unabashed praise to God, poems and hymns of adoration that He likes so much that He preserved them for publication in the Bible! Just reading one of those Psalms out loud brings me into honest, authentic praise, and that's not always easy for me as an average human being. I let the Psalmist David "prime my pump," and from there I usually move into specific prayer, asking God to help me and others who have particular needs. These requests get quite pointed, and though I don't have any trouble remembering my own special needs, I often refer to a little book in which I've written the names and sometimes the prayer requests of other people.

It's a funny thing about praying people; once you discover the power and the efficacy of prayer, you start asking other people to pray for your concerns, because you know that God wants to answer *their* prayers as well as yours! And so I'm often asked to pray for lots of other people and about lots of other situations. I don't trust my own memory, so I try to jot them down in a book—and when I don't have time to go through it point by point, I just hold up the book and say, "Lord You know the names that are written in here, and I just pray You'll meet their needs."

I believe God accepts that, and understands the intentions of my heart as well as the limitations of my time. World evangelists like Rex Humbard and Oral Roberts, who hear from millions of people in a year, *have* to use some similar means to fulfill their vows to pray for everyone who writes to them. I know those men, and how conscientious they are; when they say they'll pray over every letter and every request, they mean it; but reason says that they cannot pore over each letter individually. They must have some means of lifting up the innumerable prayer requests to God, in a collective fashion. And I believe God honors that. He's responding to individual prayer requests, as well as the intercessory prayer of the evangelist.

That's part of the immense joy of all this! We're limited, but God isn't! What we often have to do in makeshift fashion, He can perform in intimate detail! Do you remember the intense pride you felt as a little kid, knowing that your father could do things you couldn't do? And that he *wanted* to do them for you?

Well, it's just that way with God. He actually says to us, in the book of Galatians, "and because you are sons, God has sent the spirit of His Son into our hearts, crying 'Abba! Father!'" (Galatians 4:6, RSV)

Let that soak in just a minute. Sons. God has sent forth the Spirit (breath) of His Son into our hearts. You know what Father means, but what about that word "Abba"?

It means—"Daddy." It's one of the most endearing words in the Hebrew language. Are you starting to get the picture?

My evangelist friend Kenneth Copeland explains it this way: "Look, I've got two kids, and when I come in, my boy John will come running and jump on my lap and give me a hug and a kiss. He'll rummage around in my pockets and if he can find anything in them, gum or something like that, he'll say, 'Daddy, can I have this?' Or he might just say, 'Thanks, Daddy,' and go ahead and take it because he knows I'm his daddy and anything I have that's not harmful to him is his as well as mine. He may wrinkle my pants, smudge my collar, and get his sweat and grime all over me and take stuff that's in my pockets—but that's okay because he's my child and I'm his daddy.

"But if John starts misbehaving, and if he's not listening when his mother calls him or tells him to stop, and I have to get up from my chair and walk to the door and call his name loudly—he jumps to attention right now, because that's *father* talking!"

God truly wants to be Father and Daddy to you—and His Spirit/breath in you will teach you the difference. Like Tevye, the fiddler on the roof, my response to a firm but loving Father should be immediate and spontaneous and unafraid—unless I've really gotten out of line. And even then, a quick and honest "I'm sorry, Father" can set things right again.

You see? I'm not talking about religion. I'm talking about relationship! A living and breathing relationship with a loving Father/God.

Look at this verse I ran across just this morning:

> O Lord, be gracious to us;
> We long for you.
> *Be our strength every morning,*
> Our salvation in time of distress.
> > (Isaiah 33:2 New International Version)

5 The Practical Side of Private Prayer

Not everyone prays the way I do.

I expect that's just fine with God; it might get boring to Him if everybody prayed the same way.

In fact, the more I learn about this Creator/God, the more I realize He really appreciates diversity. Look at the incredible innovations and eccentricities in the world of nature, in the animal kingdom, in cloud formations and sunsets. Take a look at your own fingerprints. There are no two sets alike in the whole world! I just have a feeling, then, that He appreciates some originality in our praying.

As a result, He seems to have laid down very few rules about it. Certainly position doesn't seem to matter very much; some folks kneel, some sit with their heads bowed, many these days stand with their hands upraised and their faces uplifted, as I often do. An early church father named Tertullian always stood with his hands extended, like Jesus on the cross. Some very devout folks, especially Muslims, pray almost prostrate with their faces on the ground. I suppose the body posture ought to reflect something of the inner mood, the prompting of the human spirit, whether it's joy, reverence, grief or some kind of urgent need.

C. S. Lewis advised in his *Letters to Malcolm:* "The body ought to pray as well as the soul. Body and soul are both the better for it. Bless the body. Mine has led me into many scrapes, but I've led it into far more. . . . The relevant point is that kneeling does matter, but other things matter even more. A concentrated mind and a sitting body make for better prayer than a kneeling body and a mind half asleep."

Where you pray has something to do with it, too. As you pray more frequently, I think you'll find that you can keep a regular dialogue going with God in almost any location—whether on a roaring commuter train, on a freeway, or maybe even in the midst of a stimulating dinner-party conversation, sort of subliminally. But there are times when drawing away to some secluded spot will seem almost a necessity. Francis of Assisi spent some of the most productive hours of his life alone with God in the forests of Italy. Jesus Himself, the master prayer, recommended that we ought to go to our rooms (even our closets), shut the door and communicate with God in secret (Matthew 6:6); He promised special rewards for that kind of prayer.

Praying with others in a group setting can be socially stimulating as well as spiritually beneficial; "praying on the run" in the midst of a hectic day is a very good practice; *but private, secluded prayer is where the most intimate friendships with God grow best.*

A writer I know based in New York City told me that he had been involved for a number of years in small prayer groups and regular worship services. But when he decided to embark on a systematic program of prayer times in the morning, he felt as though he hardly knew the God to whom he was speaking. An entirely new dimension of supernatural communication opened up when he decided to meet God alone.

The place just doesn't seem to matter very much, as long as it affords privacy. There's nowhere God can't, or won't, go—especially when one of His family wants to talk to Him privately. C. S. Lewis again: "A clergyman once said to me that a railway compartment, if one has it to oneself, is an extremely good place to pray in 'because there is just the right amount of distraction.' When I asked him to explain he said that perfect silence and solitude left one more open to the distractions that come from within, and that a moderate amount of external distraction was easier to cope with. I don't find this so myself, but I can imagine it."

Time? Nothing sacred about that either. I've already told you how I like to start my day; the *amount* of time I spend depends a lot on my daily schedule, how much sleep I felt I had to have, and how fast I need to get off the starting blocks on that particular day. Whether I have five minutes or an hour, I try to get most of the ingredients I've already told you about packed in somehow, in some combination. There's no set ritual with me. There have been times when I've become so engrossed in the Scriptures that forty-five minutes have zipped by, leaving me little time to pray. When the pressures of certain problems are greater, I may abbreviate the reading and spend most of my time on my knees, in real supplication. And my conversation with the Lord doesn't end there, either—it's only just begun. I've had some pretty high-quality communication driving along in the car; sometimes, when the pressures of a rehearsal or business decisions or family problems become very intense, I'll take a quick stroll down a hall or a sidewalk and "call home"; and I almost *never* walk on a stage or in front of a TV camera without committing myself and that time (and that audience) to God. Bedtime is no exception, either; though I don't say, "Now I lay me down to sleep...," I do just feel better and sleep more soundly after a quiet "sign-off" exchange. A startling miracle happened to me early in my spiritual growth, as a result of one of those "sign-off" prayers—but I'll tell you about that later.

The greatest spiritual giants in every age have discovered one cardinal principle about prayer time, though: "more is better." The Bible records that, on some occasions, Jesus would spend entire nights in prayer. King David and the Old Testament prophet Daniel were known to pray three times a day.

In more recent times, the founder of Methodism, John Wesley, spent at least one to two hours a day in private communication with God. Both Martin Luther and Bishop Francis Asbury, the early American Methodist leader, felt that two hours of prayer a day was a minimum. If you're gasping with disbelief at this point, consider the great Scottish preacher John Welch, who regularly prayed for *eight or ten hours a day*—and often woke up in the middle of the night to continue his deep discussions with God.

Now don't think that these men were ivory-tower contemplatives who accomplished little else in their lifetimes. No, sir! These were consummate men of action who had such an impact on the affairs of human beings that they personally changed the course of history! Bishop Asbury, for example, braved a voyage from England to the fledgling United States in the late eighteenth century and then proceeded to travel about 300,000 miles, mostly on horseback, in a successful effort to build the American Methodist church up from a few hundred members to more than 200,000. Yet he, Luther, Wesley and all the other great "divine conversationalists" felt it was essential to combine earth-shaking action with lengthy, secluded prayer.

And the idea hasn't died out yet! Even in these hectic, harried times. In the world of big business, for example, you'll find that some of the most successful giants in almost any field have discovered the power of lengthy, consistent prayer times. True, their goals may be quite different, but they've tapped into the same Power Source—and we'll eavesdrop on some real prayer winners in just a few minutes.

But first, let's go back in the time machine and focus a little more closely on a couple of these spiritual giants—Martin Luther and Francis of Assisi. Luther described his own method of praying in great detail in 1535 in a letter to Peter Beskendorf, an old friend known also as "Peter the Barber." Luther had written in response to a letter from Beskendorf asking for suggestions on the best way to pray.

Luther told his friend that when he felt least inclined to pray, he usually grabbed his psalter and ran off to his room or joined people who might be worshiping in the church. In other words, he always tried to act *counter to his natural tendency not to pray* because "the flesh and the devil always prevent and hinder prayer." While alone in his room, he would repeat to himself the Ten Commandments, the Apostles' Creed, and often some saying from Christ or verses from Paul and the Psalms.

"This I do in all respects as children do," he explained.

Now I realize that Martin Luther's *business* was religion; very few of us today would have the interest or the commitment or the time to follow his example in every detail; but let's keep following him a little longer, in the chance that we may pick up a couple of practical ideas that will fit into our life-styles and commitments.

Luther was a tremendous man of action, and he never recommended that a person sit around and pray when there was work that needed to be done. But he also believed that prayer should be combined *with* work, and he recommended strongly that a man should make prayer "the first business of the morning and the last of night"—certainly a workable formula, even in the frantic 20th century.

After his heart was "warmed" by meditation on certain passages of the Bible and the creeds, he would kneel down with folded hands and lift up his eyes toward heaven. Then he would acknowledge to God that he was unworthy to speak directly to Him, but that he was about to do so because the Scriptures command us to pray. Then he suggested moving into a recitation of the Lord's Prayer and focusing on what each part of this prayer meant to him personally, as an individual.

At first, this may seem just too "religious" to you, but it's actually very practical as well as spiritually uplifting. We're human after all, every one of us, and our minds tend to wander almost beyond our control, no matter how serious we may be, no matter how urgent our needs. Martin Luther talked about that tendency in a letter to Peter the Barber: "What is it but tempting God to blabber with one's mouth and let one's mind wander? This is what the priest did who prayed: 'Make haste O God to deliver me.' Boy, hitch up the horse. 'Make haste to help me, O Lord.' Girl, go milk the cow. 'Glory be to the Father, and to the Son, and to the Holy Ghost.' Run, boy, and may the fever take you!"

He concluded that it's probably better not to pray at all than to do it with a cold, distracted mind. And he added: "a good barber has to be careful to keep his eyes on his razor and not to let his mind wander. Otherwise his friend's nose may pay the price of his distraction!"

Luther also recommended combining prayer time with reading other passages of Scripture, such as the Ten Commandments. For example, he got into the practice of reflecting on each commandment in four ways—as a teaching, an occasion of thanksgiving, a confession and a prayer of supplication. Take the First Commandment, which reads, "I am the Lord your God . . . You shall have no other gods before me." (Exodus 20:2–3, RSV) He would first focus on the *teaching* aspect, such as the importance of having confidence in God in all circumstances and relying and trusting in nothing but Him. Next, Luther would *thank* God for His divine offer to be our object of worship. Then, he might *confess* his failure to put God first in all circumstances. And finally, he would *ask* that he could understand this first commandment and live more closely in accordance with it.

Now these are great examples—but I realize they're pretty advanced for a person just exploring the possibilities of a prayer life. I hope you'll stay with me, though, for the same reason that a little league baseball player studies the life of Joe DiMaggio or Hank Aaron. The lives of champions in any field reveal the keys to success, but nobody gets there overnight. In fact, Luther himself warned, "But see to it that you do not use all of it or too much of it, lest your spirit become weary. A good prayer need not be long and should not be drawn out, but rather should be frequent and ardent. It is sufficient if you can find a portion from this, even a small portion which can strike a spark in your heart."

Another guy who has already made the first team in the all-time Prayer Hall of Fame is Francis of Assisi. This thirteenth-century saint, though born in a very wealthy family, is revered in both Protestant and Catholic circles for his simple life-style and deep love for the poor, and he accomplished an incredible amount in his forty-five years. He founded the Franciscan order, restored numerous dilapidated Italian chapels, and helped more needy people than most of us even notice in a lifetime.

He was an achiever—a real winner!

But at the same time, Francis seemed to spend most of his life in prayer. As St. Bonaventure puts it in his *Life of St. Francis*, "Whether walking or sitting, within doors or without, at toil or at leisure, he was so absorbed in prayer that he seemed to have devoted not only his whole heart and body, but also his whole heart and time." One story that Bonaventure tells to illustrate this devotion to prayer involved a trip that Francis took through the large town of Borgo. As he was riding through on an ass, many people pressed in upon him and touched his garments, but when he arrived at his destination, a lepers' settlement, some time later, he asked when they were going to get to Borgo. He had been so wrapped up on his conversation with God that he hadn't even *noticed* the passing of miles and crowds of people.

Francis also set aside a number of regular periods, or "canonical hours," during which he prayed throughout the day. And he never missed one of these "appointments with God," even though he had serious health problems with his eyes, stomach, spleen and liver. Bonaventure notes that he never even leaned against a wall when he was praying but stood bolt upright and tried to completely avoid "empty fantasies." Even if storms and rains were raging about him as he traveled on an open road, he still would not change his habit of regular communication with God.

"Hold on!" you may be asking, "are you recommending this kind of fanatic behavior for me? Forget it!"

No, I'm really not recommending that, for you or myself; I'm not there yet, and I may never be. Neither of these men was involved in the world of business; neither of them had a gold record or TV series; and I don't think either of them ever paid income tax. You and I have a totally different set of problems than they had, and perhaps different strengths and weaknesses. They *did* have weaknesses, for sure: Francis of Assisi, in spite of all his dedication and concentration, admitted that periodically his mind wandered away, and this was a source of terrific distress to him (though I'm not at all sure that it's always a bad thing—more about that later); and Martin Luther had real blind spots, including a strong anti-Semitic streak and such a legalistic approach to God and prayer that his later life appears to have been almost joyless.

No, I'm not offering either of these two men or their prayer patterns as a blueprint for you and me. I'm simply saying that two of the greatest men in recorded history became eminently successful, not in *spite* of the time they took to pray—but *because* of it! Each developed his own unique approach, and I am confident that God wants to tailor one for each of us that's just as distinctive as our fingerprints; that's just the way He works! And though we can learn something from the example of others, our own prayer lives should never be purely imitative, or static, or ritualistic. They should be growing and innovative and changing—and fun!

You heard me—prayer can and should be fun!

At the very least, it should be opposite of tedious and dull and boring. Come up with your own style! Invent! Create—that's one of your God-given characteristics.

Arthur Robertson, Associate Professor of Biblical Studies at King's College in New York, is a pretty good example of what I'm talking about. A few years back, Robertson had a tough schedule which involved taking several courses in New York City and then commuting back and forth for several hours to his upstate college campus to teach courses. He had to stay up almost all night two days a week to get all his work done.

He was so tired that he found he really couldn't

concentrate very easily on praying for his students, yet he knew he had a tremendous obligation for their intellectual and spiritual well-being. So he hit upon a technique that enabled him to keep his tired mind in focus and also made good use of the commuting time in his car every day. In short, he decided to put the names of each of his two hundred students on a cassette tape recorder, with about fifteen seconds between each name. He also interspersed a number of his favorite Bible verses on the tape. Then, as the tape rolled while he was driving, the names of each of those students would come up, with a pause on the tape so that he could pray specifically for each one as he felt the Spirit leading him.

Pretty good, huh? Prayer that involves electronic technology *and* time-space efficiency. Francis of Assisi would have been impressed! Maybe even jealous!

But even an ingenious method like this isn't foolproof. Professor Robertson found himself, ever so briefly, considering just putting his prayers on the tape and then playing both the recorded names and the recorded prayers *so that he wouldn't have to do anything at all!* "I had a good laugh with myself when that thought crossed my mind," he chuckled. "If there was ever a perfect example of the 'empty phrases' or 'vain repetition' that Jesus warned against in the Sermon on the Mount, I guess my recorded prayer fantasy would fit the bill!"

Another achievement-oriented man who relied heavily on prayer was my friend Art DeMoss, the founder and President of the National Liberty Corporation, the most successful mail-order insurance business in the nation. Art said, "I accepted a challenge about twenty-five years ago to give God the first hour each day, primarily in prayer and Scripture reading. I have found this to be the most valuable thing I do. The busier I get, the more I feel the need for this time with the Lord at the start of the day."

Art DeMoss got up at about six o'clock and actually spent more like an hour and a half each day in this period of supernatural communication. He devoted about one-third of his time to reading the Scriptures and the other two-thirds to prayer, mostly for hundreds of individuals he knew who hadn't "tuned in" yet, who were floundering through life on their own. He read the Scripture at a steady pace, without any meditation during this morning session.

"I'll study and meditate under different circumstances," he explained.

Specifically, Art told me he read one chapter of Proverbs, five Psalms and two chapters consecutively from each of the Old and New Testaments. This approach enabled him to go through the Old Testament once a year, the New Testament three times a year, and the Psalms and Proverbs once each month. "I've found this plan very helpful," he said, "because we have in the Proverbs the greatest wisdom and in the Psalms the most radiant, jubilant, exuberant literature ever penned since the dawn of creation."

At various times Art kept a written prayer list, but the more he prayed, "the more the list became a part of my mind," he explained. A steady stream of individuals and concerns came into his mind over a period of about an hour, including missionaries, Christian leaders, friends, 'lost' people, and even enemies."

Did I hear you saying, "an hour and a half—praying? I'm a busy man! I can't *afford* to spend my time that way—" Art DeMoss said he couldn't afford *not* to!

"It's important to start with God before you get involved with others," Art said. "By praying early in the morning and then at various times throughout the day when there's some personal encounter or an important decision to be made, I've found that *I think much more clearly*—prayer clears away the cobwebs and enables me to be more decisive in making judgments." He said that his business, which included five insurance companies which did several hundred million dollars in sales each year, had been built "almost totally on faith and prayer. I've never had any visions or heard God speak audibly, but I think God influences my thinking and helps me to make the right decisions. What we have to do is to really get ourselves 'in neutral' and seek His will rather than our own. If you can get yourself out of the way and genuinely seek to find the will of God, He can shape your thinking and lead you to the right kind of decisions. We don't always know exactly what God's will is, but if we can just decide that we *want* it, whatever it is, it's easier to ascertain His will and come much closer to it."

These are the words of a highly successful businessman—who prayed to win!

Just a few days after I'd written this report about Art DeMoss, he died suddenly at the age of fifty-three. At his home outside Philadelphia, playing tennis with some of his kids and as radiantly happy as he'd ever been in his life, he was instantly ushered out of this life into the next. Why this sudden stunning transition took place, only God himself knows. But ask yourself this question, as I have: if your life on this earth ended in the next moment, wouldn't you love to have had the daily preparation that Art DeMoss had?

6 Prerequisites for Prayer Power

Prayer is a language.

Just like English, or Greek, or Japanese or Hindustani. Of course, you can pray in any language known to man— and many people these days are even praying in languages *unknown* to man! The Bible talks about speaking to God "with the tongues of men and of angels," opening up very intriguing possibilities. We'll talk about that later.

But prayer *itself* is a language, a distinct form of supernatural communication. Think about it; if it works at all, if a person can speak words into the air and somehow those words are received by an eternal Creator/Being, then a miracle has occurred; an entrance has been made into another dimension, a supernatural realm. Obviously, the language of prayer doesn't conform to any natural law.

But it can be learned, and it can be highly successful, with the results largely predictable—because there are certain elemental ground rules that govern it. Yes, we've already seen that God wants us to be original, and spontaneous, and that the most naive prayer probe can get through. But I still believe that to be a consistent, triumphant winner in prayer, there are some basic fundamentals that need to be learned, understood and practiced. These ideas are not just off the top of my head; they've been culled out by years of study and experience, trial and error—and at the risk of seeming presumptious, I'll list them for you.

1. You must ask. Does this sound self-evident, maybe even silly? Well, maybe so—but I'm constantly amazed at the number of people who want God to respond to them but for some reason fail to approach Him. James, the half-brother of Jesus, wrote, "You do not have, because you do not ask." (James 4:2, RSV) And I've heard many people express this idea: "Oh, it's fine to ask for God's blessing and wisdom, and make rather general prayers about the condition of the world and things like that, always saying, 'but Thy will be done.' But God's too big and too busy for us to bother Him with any of our little personal needs, or to ask Him for anything really *specific*—"

Wrong.

The Scriptures take the exact opposite approach, and so have the greatest exponents of prayer throughout the ages. Jesus, for example, instructed us through the Lord's Prayer to ask for our daily *bread*. In His world-famous Sermon on the Mount, he offered *many* insights into God's interest in our daily affairs and our personal need, materially and spiritually. And then, for His whole three-year ministry on earth, He went around *demonstrating* God's interest in all the things that interest us—He healed the sick whenever they asked Him to, He fed the hungry, He produced the money for His disciples to pay their taxes, *He responded to every request ever made of Him!* Then He turned around and in several places urged us to "ask *anything* in My name" and expect His Father to answer! How explicit and specific can you be?

But it starts with asking.

So don't limit the subject matter that you pray about, because if you do, you're sure to miss out on many of the benefits and blessings that God has already set aside for you in this life. The Bible says that He knows every sparrow that falls, and He's counted the hairs on your head—and if He's that interested in all the intimate details of your life (and He is), don't assume that any subject is too small or personal to discuss with Him in prayer.

Ask! What in the world have you got to lose?

2. *Give God your complete attention.* How do you like it when you're talking to somebody, and he or she is constantly looking at a watch or at other people in the room? When a person is so distracted by other things or other thoughts that he continually asks you to repeat what you said, still without listening very closely, does it irritate you just a little? Don't you wonder why you're talking to that person in the first place? I have to believe that since God is a Person, He must be similarly disappointed when I don't focus completely on our communication. *The Catholic Encyclopedia* actually says, "attention is the very essence of prayer; as soon as this attention ceases, prayer ceases." I suspect this may be true—and I must have "hung up" on God a lot of times. Fortunately for me, He doesn't hang up on His end of the line!

And remember—*listening* is one of the sincerest forms of attention. Expressing specific requests is an absolute must, but sitting quietly and listening in your spirit for some answer from God may bring the quickest and surest results. Don't assume you're too imperfect or insensitive to hear from the Lord, as I often have; if God considers you important enough to *listen* to you, chances are He'll *say* something to you, too. In fact, Jesus said in John 10:27, "My sheep, hear my voice!" Expect it; be attentive; listen.

3. *Be sincere.* Don't waste your time trying to "snow" God. It won't work. He calls that hypocrisy, and He hates it.

"O God, help me!" "Lord, be merciful to me; I'm a sinner." "Lord, I can't figure this out. Why is this happening to me?"

"Father, to be honest with You, I really don't feel much like praying right now. I'm tired, and bugged, and pretty fed up with the way things are going. Can I just sit here and think about things, and listen for anything You might want to tell me?"

Friend, I'm not trying to put words in your mouth. But the Bible tells us that God knows what we need *before* we even ask for it, so there's absolutely no value in high-sounding rhetoric or any other phony ploys. He just wants you to level with Him, as you would with your most intimate friend. That's what He is.

4. *Love should be the primary environment in which you pray.*

Can you imagine God responding to this kind of prayer? "Lord, I want You to really punish old Joe for what he did to me. He may be richer and more powerful than I am, but I know You can get him, and I pray You'll really cut him down. Amen."

Or this? "Father, I'm just so thankful that You didn't make me as hypocritical and ugly and unlikable as Mabel Mertz. If You want to bless her, it's okay with me, but she's one poor excuse for a human being."

No, even a rank beginner will sense that these prayers aren't likely to get out of the room, much less to the heart of God. Common sense should tell us that if God loves any of us enough to take the time and care to listen to our petitions, that He probably cares just as much for all the rest of us. Spoiled brats don't usually become winners. In fact, the whole message of the Bible is that God loves everyone of us with such an indescribable love that He was willing to lay His life down and die for us—each and every one of us! So prayer that really gets results must dip down into that kind of love, and come up the same color. And that color is blood red.

That kind of love is called *agape* in the New Testament, and is the highest form of love there is. It's not sensual, it may not necessarily be emotional, it's not materialistic—it's a kind of motivating force that literally desires the good of the other person above our own. And that's not easy to come by! You can't "work it up," and you can't buy it. In a sense it's free, but it cost God everything, and the only way you can get it is *to have God inside you*, generating love from within.

Does that sound mystical? I guess it is, but so is solar heating. I really don't understand much about that, but I'm told you can put some glass plates, sort of like windows on your roof—and the sunlight will heat up some elements in the glass, which will in turn transfer some heat down into your basement somewhere, and then warm water will flow up through the rooms of your house and keep everybody inside nice and warm. But unless you put those windowlike panels on your roof, the sunlight will just bounce off the tiles, and you can all get pretty cold and uncomfortable inside if you want to. Lots of folks these days are getting interested in sun power.

Lots of folks are getting interested in Son power, too. Jesus, the Son of God, said awesome things like this: "I am the Light of the world. No man can come to the Father except through Me. There is no greater love than this, that a man would lay down his life for a friend. You are My friend, if you keep My commandments. If you remain in Me and My words remain in you, ask whatever you wish, and it will be given you. As the Father has loved Me, so will I love you. Now remain in My love. My command is this: love each other as I have loved you." (Most of this is found in the 15th chapter of the Gospel of John.)

Jesus taught—and demonstrated—the greatest kind of love there is. And there's only one way to get that kind of love operating in your own life, and in your prayers. He is the way. He's the solar panel, the window which must be incorporated into your physical dwelling, through which God's own love can penetrate and permeate and transform your inner being. Until that happens, you're on the outside looking in, begging for a favor from the King.

But *after* it happens, you're inside the house, part of the family and asking for your share of the Father's provision. And *"we receive from Him whatever we ask because we keep His commandments and do what pleases Him. And this is His commandment, that we should believe in the name of His Son Jesus Christ and love one another just as He has commanded us."*

Do you get my point? The kind of love that tugs at the heart of God, the kind that produces real results is the kind of love that puts the other guy first, and truly *accepts* the ultimate loving gift of His own Son's life!

And this love demonstrates itself in very practical, very readable ways. You can always tell whether you have it or not by the way your human relationships are doing. For example, if you're having problems with your spouse, it may be that God's love has leaked out of that area of your life. And the Apostle Peter warns in 1 Peter 3:7 that problems in the marital relationship may cause a man's own prayers to "be hindered," the answers to be blocked.

71

So God's love, His *agape* kind of love comes first. Now then, what was that you were asking for?

5. Approach God with a clean and forgiving heart. This may sound impractical, and almost impossible, but once the love starts operating, anything can happen! In fact, it's very hard for selfishness and unforgiveness to exist in the rarefied atmosphere of real love.

May I give you another personal example? A couple of years ago, I had a very emotional encounter with former Black Panther leader Eldridge Cleaver, soon after his "born again" experience. He had just returned to this country and had been hit with criminal charges for some of his alleged previous activities. Some mutual friends thought we ought to meet, so Shirley and I invited Eldridge, his wife Kathleen, along with George and Virginia Otis, to our home for dinner. All four of our daughters were home then, so we filled up every one of the seats around the big circular table in the family room of our home.

After some pleasantries and some awkward attempts at getting acquainted, we all sat down around the table and joined hands to pray before we ate. Just as we were about to bow our heads, Eldridge volunteered a statement, sort of a "confession," which began a very meaningful prayer experience for us all.

"This is just blowing my mind," he told us. "I can remember some of my buddies in L.A. coming around and looking at this house and others in Beverly Hills. We were sizing it up, planning to break into this place, y'know? Of course that never happened, but here we are in this same house—getting ready to pray together. It's just blowing my mind."

Deeply moved, I looked over at him and said, "Since it's true confession time, I'll tell you it's blowing my mind too—because I nearly took Debby out of school when a teacher assigned her *Soul on Ice* to read. I had read it, and even though I admired your intelligence and sympathized with some of the things you were trying to say, I didn't think this was a book for any fifteen-year-old girl, with the language and explicit sexual dreams you talked about."

"You're right," he said. "She shouldn't have read it. Some of the things I said then I still think are valid, but a lot was just lost babbling, and I regret it."

Then it was Shirley's turn: "It's equally 'mind-boggling' to me that after all this background you're a welcome guest here in our home and we're joining hands to pray. Not only that—we *love* you! Only God could have brought this about."

Still joining hands, we bowed, and Eldridge Cleaver led us to the throne of God in prayer. It was a simple, honest and eloquent statement of his gratitude, his love and his wonder, his request for God's blessings for all of us. I added some prayer of my own, but I really felt that Eldridge had already touched all the bases. He certainly touched our hearts. And after dinner we all wound up on our knees in our den, praying and weeping together and praising God with the kind of joy I've rarely experienced before. Though a transformed personality is always a miracle, we had that special sense that Eldridge and Kathleen's experience was particularly dramatic and awesome—a sovereign act of an all-powerful, all-loving God.

Jesus, an expert on forgiveness *and* prayer, knowing already that He was to be crucified as an innocent victim, issued this directive: "And whenever you stand praying, forgive, if you have anything against any one; so that your Father also who is in heaven may forgive you your trespasses." (Mark 11:25, RSV) He made forgiveness—unconditional forgiveness—an absolute prerequisite to unlimited, triumphant, success-oriented prayer. And that's not easy, is it? Forgiveness is pretty tough for most of us. But Jesus didn't stop there; coming at the problem from the viewpoint of the *other* guy, He instructed, in Matthew 5:23–24, that before we try to worship (or pray), we should first be reconciled to anyone who might have something against us! That is, if you know that somebody has unforgiveness toward you—that you should go to him and try to work it out with him, to initiate some kind of settlement. For me, that's even a tougher assignment.

But it is essential. *More prayers are blocked and neutralized by unforgiveness than just about anything else.* That bitter feeling is not worth much anyway, and it's certainly not worth missing God's richest blessings. So, if you're really serious about being a prayer champion, make a quality decision to erase unforgiveness from your heart, and ask God to help you. Amazingly, He will.

David summed it up pretty well in Psalm 66:18–19, RSV: "If I had cherished iniquity in my heart, the Lord would not have listened. But truly God has listened; he has given heed to the voice of my prayer."

6. *Be persistent and diligent as you pray.* Dabbling will get you nowhere. You can't get to be a champion miler by jogging once a week; you don't become immensely successful in business by making occasional phone calls to prospective customers; you don't elect a political candidate by sending out some random mailings from time to time.

We're talking about *winning;* about achieving goals; about success in life, both materially and spiritually. These are objectives worthy of the highest and most diligent commitment—and that's exactly what they require.

I keep using Jesus as an example, because there was never a more powerful prayer champion in human history than the man from Galilee. Our calendars are dated now from His birth, throughout the world, and though He only physically inhabited a few square miles during a brief lifetime, and most of the world didn't know He existed, He has emerged as the most significant single figure in the history of this planet! And prayer is the path He trod. He is Chairman Emeritus of the school of prayer, and He emphasized how important it is to keep up a consistent barrage of prayers over a long period of time if you hope to achieve maximum results. One of the parables He told to illustrate this point involved a fellow who knocked on his friend's door at midnight to ask for three loaves of bread to feed an unexpected visitor. At first, the friend refused, saying it was too late and his kids were all asleep. But finally, because of the insistence of the fellow outside—not simply because of their friendship—the sleepy friend inside got up and gave the other guy what he needed. On another occasion, Jesus told a story of an unjust judge, who initially refused a widow who wanted to be vindicated against her adversary. But because she kept after him, he decided, "Though I neither fear God nor regard man, yet *because this widow bothers me,* I will vindicate her, or she will wear me out by her continual coming." (Luke 11:5–8; 18:1–8)

God Himself is consistent; He is persistent; He never gives up His own objectives. And I think He wants to encourage the same qualities in us. He may very well want to see just how serious we are about our goals, how conscientious we're willing to be in achieving them. And then, there's always the matter of waiting for and developing the right timing. There are always good reasons when we don't get what we ask for exactly when we ask; but the last thing we should do is give up.

A young lady called me on my home phone one evening. I was just about to sit down with the family for dinner when the answering service operator rang and mentioned that someone whose name sounded very familiar to me was trying to reach me.

It wasn't a very convenient time to take the call, but I decided, since I thought I knew the person, that I'd go ahead and accept it. To my dismay, it turned out not to be the person I had expected, but just a stranger with a similar name who had called my office after office hours. But I was on the line now, and thinking it might not be an accident after all, I agreed to listen to her story. She said she was calling from Atlanta and explained, "My friend is on drugs and I don't know what to do about it."

She said she was rooming with a girl who was threatening to kill herself, "But I can't seem to get through to her—she won't listen to me. She gets very angry. I don't know where to turn, but I recently read one of your books, and I just wanted to call and ask you to pray for this person," she pleaded.

"Okay, I will," I replied. "But I want *you* to pray for her too. Are you a Christian?"

"Yes," she said.

"And you believe in prayer?"

"Yes."

"Well then, we'll agree together in prayer right now on the phone for your friend," I said. "I'll continue to pray for her, and you do it too because the Bible says we should keep praying for people and circumstances that need to be changed. But let me give you a little tip here. *I've never suggested this to anybody*, but it just occurred to me. I've been reading 2 Timothy 2:24–26, RSV, where it says that God's servant mustn't get involved in quarrels and arguments, but should pray that *God* will operate on people who are angry and deceived, so that 'they may escape from the snare of the devil. . . .'

"Well, the picture that I get is that those who are very stubborn—who are involved in things that are very bad for them but they can't give up—are caught in a kind of snare because the devil has deluded and trapped them. No amount of arguing is going to get them out of there. They'll thrash around in their web or trap and lash out at *you*. So just pray for your friend and don't be surprised if she snaps back and accuses you of things you haven't done. Remember, she's caught in the 'devil's snare.' But as you start praying, God's going to release her from within. As she goes through this process of being released from satanic control, she may do some very unkind things toward you, but *don't let that stop you from praying*. In fact, be encouraged and take it as a sign that you're getting through!"

She agreed to take this approach. After we prayed briefly on the phone together, we hung up; and I really didn't think I would hear from her again. Ten days or so went by, and I prayed about her friend a few times; finally, the concern just drifted out of my thinking. But then I got a phone call from that same girl while I was at the office. She was beside herself with excitement.

"My friend has quit taking drugs!" she exclaimed. "She's wandering around like she's in a daze, like she doesn't know what's happened to her, but she's *free!*"

"I guess you really prayed for her," I commented.

"Oh, I was praying three and four hours a day," she replied.

"You were?" I exclaimed, surprised by the incredible commitment she had made to her friend.

"Yes, I went on about my work, but during work and after work, I just kept praying and praying and praying for her. But boy, it's a good thing you warned me!"

"What do you mean?" I asked.

"Because after about two days while I was praying for her, she went completely nutty and accused me of stealing some stuff of hers. I never saw her so angry; she was violent. I thought she was going to slap me or even strangle me. She was furious at me several times after that and came so close to hitting me that I really became frightened. If you hadn't warned me, I guess I might have said, 'Well, I've been praying for you, but forget it, if that's the way you're going to act.'"

"Yes, that's exactly what the devil wanted to accomplish," I said. "You see, you were making him squirm, and he knew he was going to have to let her go unless he could get you to quit praying."

"Well, she's free now, but it wasn't anything I said or did to her," the girl said. "When she accused me of those things, I just kept my mouth shut and kept praying."

Isn't that intriguing? I don't know about you, but it really excites me. This girl really *committed* herself to pray for her friend, and she wasn't going to quit until she got the job done. It took about ten days—which is more than most people would invest, without seeing results—but through the dynamic of prayer she accomplished more than a team of psychiatrists, a rehabilitation hospital, and the Bureau of Narcotics could have done in a year!

Other goals take longer—a lot longer.

My friend Arthur DeMoss of the National Liberty Corporation frequently felt moved to pray for those who had not established a relationship with the Lord. On one occasion, he discussed his faith with the president of a company in the Midwest and then began to pray for this man *every day for a total of twelve years.*

"I had no further contact with him by mail or anything, but when I was out in Detroit one day on business, I got a phone call in my hotel room," DeMoss recalled. "It was this company president, and he wanted to know if we could get together. While we talked later that day, he prayed and accepted Christ because he felt a need had developed in his life over the past few years."

On another occasion, DeMoss actually prayed for a former business partner *for twenty-seven years,* and finally the man decided in a telephone conversation with DeMoss to commit his life to Christ. Right away, his whole life changed.

"There are things I don't understand, but I do know God doesn't keep time the way we do," Art told me. "One day is a thousand years for God. It's all the same to Him. But we tend to get discouraged. We pray for something or someone a few times and then give up or drop it. But it's exciting to see answers to prayer like this, where God softens and prepares another person's heart over a period of years. I'm confident that many of the people we meet along life's way are people that others have been praying for—and I'm also sure that many people I don't even know or remember are praying for me and helping to deepen my relationship with God."

Still with me?

Is all this beginning to sound like work? Well, I suppose, in the highest sense it is. It's not backbreaking labor, but it is "Kingdom business." Do you remember the Lord's Prayer? One of the basic things Jesus prayed for, in His example to us of how we should pray, was "Thy Kingdom come, thy will be done on earth, as it is in heaven." And for two thousand years, God has been steadily advancing His Kingdom on this planet, establishing branch offices and bringing in new personnel all the time. You don't have to punch a clock, usually, and there are no accredited unions, but the pension and profit-sharing plan is fabulous! The retirement benefits just won't quit—in fact they're eternal! But the training is on-the-job, and there's lots of room for advancement. Success and rewards really depend on the desire and persistence and commitment of the individual associate; and the real advantage is that the Chairman of the Board makes each of us His full partner!

I'm not trying to be cute, and I won't stretch the

analogy any further. But the truth is that all these things we've just talked about will be very important to you in attaining your own personal goals through prayer.

And now, the three most important principles of all. In addition to the six points we've already made, if you really want to move into the top echelon of prayer people, THE WINNER'S CIRCLE, these next three principles are absolutely essential. Without them, I believe your attempts at prayer are doomed to be hit-or-miss affairs.

7. *Pray in Jesus' name.* No, I'm not trying to get completely "religious," or convert you to anything. I'm just talking straight to you in presenting the three major keys to powerful and winning prayer.

Jesus said in John 14:13–14, "Whatever you ask in My name, I will do it, that the Father may be glorified in the Son; if you ask anything in My name, I will do it." (RSV) But asking in His name does not mean just tacking on "in Christ's name" at the end of each prayer, like some magic incantation. In fact, Jesus Himself said that not everyone who calls on His name will necessarily get what he asks for. (Matthew 7:21) The important thing is to realize that Jesus, as God in the flesh, became the channel for men and women to establish a personal relationship with God. He's the Boss' Son! We must be in this channel—or in Christ or abiding in Christ, as the Scriptures put it—if we expect God to hear our prayers on any sort of consistent basis.

We'll discuss this more later, and handle some of the reasons in more detail—but right now I'll just give you the hard facts.

To pray "in the name of Jesus" means to pray out of a total involvement with Him. A halfway, lukewarm conditional commitment won't do. Church membership in itself isn't even enough. No, at some point or well-defined period in your life, you've got to confront the claims of the Bible head-on and decide to commit or recommit every area of your life to the "Word made flesh," to the God who was manifested in Christ. Then— you can sign His name at the bottom of the check. Using the words "in Jesus' name," can't be a rote recitation of just another traditional phrase. Oh no; every time we bow our heads or fall to our knees, and begin to communicate through that supernatural channel that Jesus has established, we must be sure that our commitment to Him is firm and vital or we're likely to find that we're not talking on God's wavelength.

Forging checks is not only criminal, it's a sin.

8. *Pray in faith.* "Now it happens; now we get religious, right?" you might ask.

Wrong.

"But faith and religion are the same thing, aren't they?" No, most of the time they're not. People have worked up all kinds of religious systems, and all kinds of doctrinal theology, and there's a good deal of truth mixed in there somewhere—but too often, if there's any faith at all involved, it's faith in the *system* or faith in the *theology*. And that's not what I'm talking about.

Faith is believing something. Faith is believing something so strongly that you'll act on that belief, perhaps even to the point of staking your life on it. Lots of people have faith in money; others have faith in politics and political systems; others have faith in raw power, criminal or otherwise; others have faith in their own charm and personality and ability. You can have faith in anything, or in nothing.

But when it comes to winning through prayer, *you've got to have faith in God, and in His Word.* If He says it, then it's so, and that's that. You can act on it, and you can stake your life on it. He says Himself in His manufacturer's handbook, "Faith comes by hearing, and hearing by the Word of God." And that's the name of that tune! There's absolutely no shortcut.

So how do you get faith? Not by trying to "work it up," by what C. S. Lewis calls "psychological gymnastics." Not necessarily by attending church, though that can certainly be very helpful. Not by just trying to straighten up your life and "being a good boy." No, if you want to have the kind of faith that really gets the job done, that fuels prayer power that can move mountains, you'll have to dust off that old Bible, open it up and let God give you some of the raw goods of His own spoken and written Word. I always recommend that my friends get hold of a good modern translation of the Bible, as much as I love the old King James Version, so that they can understand God's Word in a sort of conversational way. The truth is the same, but it's just easier to comprehend and put into today's context. Then, if you erase that imaginary two-thousand-year-old barrier between the time the ink dried on the original pages and the time the Bible you're holding was printed—you're in for more excitement than a roller coaster or a free-fall parachute drop. God makes astounding promises in His Bible, and there's no time limit on them! In addition, He gives lots of examples of the way they work. And when you start reading about ordinary men and women who defeated armies, became fabulously wealthy and powerful and influential, who ministered resurrection life to dying people, who used the simple words of God and the blank checks He handed out with those words to change the history of the world—you'll start wanting a little of that action yourself, and your prayers will begin to reflect the gold nuggets of truth that you've just mined out of God's Word!

As your faith grows, and your prayer life takes on a new dimension proportionately, you'll start experiencing a companionship with God and victories in your life that you scarcely thought possible. And, still based on the rock-like promise of His own Word, the Lord will start sharing special, intimate things with you that will astound you.

Let me tell you a startling story about a friend of mine, an editor in New York.

He was just returning on a bus from visiting a sick friend in a Manhattan hospital, when he had a strong sense that he and his wife needed to get away from the city for a brief vacation, just to renew their spirits. His wife had been working quite hard and so had he, and he couldn't remember the last time they had taken off a complete weekend just to relax.

The problem was that they didn't have enough money at the time to get away, and this depressed him. But as he sat there on that bus he had a strong sense that God was telling him, "I know you're tired and you want to get away, so I'm going to provide the means. You just tell me what you want, and I'll give it to you."

(In the Bible, God promises to do this kind of thing— and my friend *knew* these promises.)

It wasn't a voice, but rather a strong, definite impression that a warm, loving Father was concerned for him and was letting him know that his wishes would become reality when he uttered a prayer. When your relationship with God has grown to the place where you feel His presence, and recognize His voice within you—and you *know* from His Word and your experience in acting on it how He really feels about you—inward conversation like this is possible. So my friend simply said, "Thanks, Lord. We'd like to go to Bermuda for a few days, so I pray that You'll give us the means."

Within three days, this man's accountant called him and said he had made a $1,500 mistake on his income tax, so he could expect a refund in that amount. That was enough to cover a trip to Bermuda and to have a considerable amount left over besides.

It's possible that at first this story may offend your sensibilities. It may seem too crass, too reminiscent of images of God as Santa Claus.

But wait a minute! Over and over, Jesus kept insisting, "ask *anything* in My name, and My Father will do it for you." Another time He said, "Your Father knows what you need before you ask." Again, "If you abide in Me, and My words abide in you, you can ask what you *will*"! If you believe that, you'll do it!

And that's what faith is: believing and asking on God's Word.

If we could accept God as our Father, way down deep inside, we'd realize God created this world for us, just as surely as a man might build a business and turn it over to his son. He wants us to understand it in every detail, and wants us to have complete mastery over it. But it requires growth, and like many a loving parent, God requires that each of us "start at the bottom" and "grow up" through the various departments, learning a lot by trial and error, through reading His Handbook, taking on more and more responsibility, and finally arriving at the place where we can actually run the business—at least in partnership with Him!

One of the great things that Jesus did during His time on earth as a human being was to show us how *all* human beings are supposed to live! He walked on the water, was impervious to illness, fed five thousand people with a little boy's borrowed lunch, spoke to the wind and storms and hushed them instantly—and whether you're ready to believe it or not, God wants us to grow into that power dimension.

But just as you can't turn your child loose in a car until he's old enough to drive, neither can God trust us

84

with elemental power until we're mature and experienced enough to handle it properly. That's a greater responsibility than most of us can even imagine. Once, Jesus' own disciples got all upset because He wasn't being received well in the Galilee region, and they asked Him if they could call down fire from heaven to destroy several of the villages they'd just left. They had already tasted some of His kind of power—and they wanted to use it to vent their anger and frustration. Jesus jerked them up short, saying, "You don't know what Spirit you're of." I feel He was saying to them, "I can't trust you with My kind of power yet because you're still too human, too immature. You'll have to grow to the point where you realize that the strongest thing you can do for an enemy *is to pray for him*—not to curse him."

God's Word is a gold mine—and the nuggets that you dig out personally will bring you power and a greatly increased net worth. Faith is the natural by-product, and winning prayer is fueled by faith.

And the value of gold is going up every day.

9. *Pray according to God's will.* This is the heaviest, most far-reaching principle of them all.

When you fly a plane, there are lots of natural and technical laws that come into play, but the bedrock principle is the law of gravity. Praying in a way that's consistent with God's will is like that.

The implications are so varied and vital that I'm going to devote the whole next chapter to them.

7 Battle of Wits, Wisdom and Will

"Daddy, soon I'll be sixteen years old. I'd like to have a car of my own—and since two of my friends are going to get Corvettes, I'd like to have a Mercedes convertible. I know I can't get my license until after my birthday, but I hate for my friends to get their cars before I get mine. So will you go ahead and buy me my Mercedes right now, and let me keep it in the garage and maybe drive it just a little when the police aren't looking, so that none of my friends can say they were first?

"Thanks, Daddy; you're the best Daddy in the whole world!"

What do you think of that kind of request? What do you think of the father who would grant such a request? Does the whole scene seem pretty farfetched to you? Well, it is—but it actually has happened in our neighborhood! When my girls were just arriving at the age where they could get their drivers licenses and wistfully dream about having their own cars, several of their friends were actually given brand new cars by their parents and expected not to drive them but to just show them off to their friends—so that they could be "first" in their circles.

I really felt sorry for those kids.

They were being motivated totally by selfishness and juvenile pride, and their parents were just selfish and immature enough to encourage their own children that way. The fathers probably felt that by indulging their kids they were the most thoughtful and generous parents, and would therefore wind up "first" in that category, as their kids wanted to be in their own.

What's that got to do with praying in God's will? Everything. The primary thing I want you to see is that *God is willing to be your Father.* And then, as your loving and wise Father, *He wants the very best for you.* And if these two things are true, you have to admit the corollary: kids don't always know what's best for them!

The wise and truly loving parent often has to say "No"—or "wait."

I was talking once to Bob Ringer, author of the huge bestsellers *Looking Out for Number One* and *Winning Through Intimidation,* and the subject was power; we were concentrating for the moment on spiritual power, which I believe is generated and demonstrated through effective prayer. Bob confided that when he was a young boy, though not particularly religious, he did pray a number of times, and felt that God had heard him and answered his prayers. "Still, as I got on into my late teens, I prayed for some things that were pretty important to me—and nothing happened. So I just gave up the whole idea. Sort of outgrew it, I guess. What do you say to that?"

"Do you have kids?" I asked. He answered that he had four.

"Do you give them everything they ask for, when they ask for it?"

Bob grinned, and acknowledged that he didn't. "In fact," he said, "I've just been thinking recently that I'm glad my success didn't come earlier in my life. I wanted very much to be a successful author when I was in my twenties, but if it had happened then, I don't think I could have handled it. Now that I'm in my forties, I think I can handle the success and all the things that go with it in a more mature way."

"That's the way God has to deal with us," I told him. "Most of us want a lot of things, and probably most of those things are good in themselves. *But*—money and power and influence, almost every *thing* that we might want, brings with it some kind of responsibility. The greater the goals, the greater the maturity required to cope with them properly. And maturity only comes through knowledge and experience. Because God truly loves us, and because He's infinitely wiser than we are, He *can't* give us everything we ask for, right when we ask for it—any more than you can with *your* kids!"

Bob and I enjoyed our conversation, only one of many, and he dropped me a nice note later, thanking me for helping him to begin to think of God as a Father, and not some wispy ephemeral force or hoary old dictator who makes life miserable for us by issuing a lot of impossible commands that we can't keep. And that's what I wish *everybody* could come to understand; that was the whole reason that Jesus came! After four thousand years of recorded history, man still didn't understand that we are *created* beings, and that God isn't looking for a race of robots; He wants *sons* and *daughters*, capable and mature and successful and fulfilled in every way growing up to be the kind of people He can trust with governing all the rest of His creation.

I truly believe that, in a very real sense, God is like the Chairman of the Board who founded the company and who wants to bring His sons up through the structure he created, learning the business from the ground up, eventually reaching the place where they can take over, completely! He doesn't just want to give them occasional raises and bonuses and promotions—He wants to make them full-fledged partners and put the thing in their hands, still under His benign and wise counsel. As evidence of that, His number one Son, the carpenter from Nazareth, accomplished more in His life, achieving total manhood and lordship over all things in a very short lifetime, than anyone else in history—or all the rest of us put together! And I'm going to share with you (what He shares freely) the secret of His success: *He only and always did His Father's will.* He made statements like this, as simply and directly as anyone could, "For I have come here from heaven to do the will of God who sent Me, not to have My own way." "I live by the power of the living Father who sent Me, and in the same way those who partake of Me shall live because of Me!" "I'm not teaching you my own thoughts, but those of God who sent Me. If any of you really determines to do God's will, then you will certainly know whether My teaching is from God or is merely My own."

In His famous prayer, the one we call The Lord's Prayer, given as an example of how we ought to pray, He speaks these vital words: "Thy Kingdom come, *Thy will be done,* on earth as it is in heaven." Even in the anguish of the Garden of Gethsemane, as He was about to offer His life for all mankind, He knelt and asked God if there was some way, any way, to avoid the torture of the cross. His anguish was so great that blood oozed from His pores. And still, right down to the bitter dregs of His sacrificial life, He uttered, "Nevertheless, not My will, but Thine be done." And then He went through the agony of that mock trial and excruciating death on the cross. *And He came back from that Jewish grave a winner!* The greatest winner of all times, becoming the pivotal figure in all of human history! He accomplished every one of His goals, and in His resurrection from the dead and His ascension into heaven, He triumphed over death and hell forever, utterly defeating God's adversary Satan and his diabolic army for all time, and ushered you and me into a whole new dimension of triumphant living. True, our petty goals may not be the same as His, but that's not my point. He won big, He won completely—and He did it by discovering and praying the will of His Father!

Success comes through submission.

Winning, ultimately, doesn't come through intimidation—it comes through *imitation*. Imitation of the biggest winner who ever existed.

Am I talking about "religion" now? No, I'm not! I'm talking about accomplishing *your* objectives, reaching *your* goals, winning *your* victories! Jesus has already won your battle over death, if you accept His free offer. He's already won your right to have authority over the same devils that He defeated, and dominion over all creation. So you don't have to do that in your lifetime; now He wants to help you with *your* goals! But the secret of success is still the same—it has to be done in harmony with God's will through prayer. The promises are staggering:

> . . . this is the confidence which we have in Him, that if we ask *anything* according to his will, he hears us. And if we know that he hears us in whatever we ask, we know that we have obtained

90

the requests made of him. (1 John 5:14–15) (RSV)

Listen to me! You can pray for *anything*, and *if you believe, you have it*; it's yours! (Mark 11:24) (Living Bible)

In solemn truth I tell you, anyone believing in Me shall do the same miracles I have done, and *even greater ones*, because I am going to be with the Father. You can ask Him for *anything*, using My name, and I will do it, for this will bring praise to the Father because of what I, the Son, will do for you. Yes, ask *anything*, using My name, and I will do it. (John 14: 12–14) (Living Bible)

Do you begin to get the idea that God really wants us to ask Him *anything*, and that He's eager to help us with it? It's true—and it's the premise of this whole book! But there has to be a partnership, there has to be a growth, there has to be a developing relationship with the Chairman of the Board, who founded the business and who knows how it all works best. So effective prayer, winning and triumphant prayer, must incorporate and harmonize the expressed will of God.

How do you know what that is?

He has revealed it, utterly and completely, in the Bible. That's why I call it the Manufacturer's Handbook. I've already told you it's a gold mine, and that you have to dig the truths out yourself, like precious nuggets or ingots of that gold metal. Actually, truth is far better than gold, because even gold eventually falls to dust—but God's Word, His revealed will, is eternal. Any life or goal that is wrapped up with *that* commodity is going to endure!

That's why Art DeMoss started his day with Bible reading. That's why the Chairman of J. C. Penney and of the Arthur Young & Co. accounting firm, and the President of the Exxon Corporation, and so many other dynamic and successful executives spend time soaking up the wisdom of the Bible; in that black book, they find the distilled wisdom of the ages, the "how-tos" for any situation, no matter how complex, and the revealed will of God, which helps them to pray knowledgeably toward the accomplishing of their objectives.

You may call it religion—I call it practicality. It works!

Say you want to fly a plane. Is it enough that you can afford to buy one? Is it enough that you can walk out to the airstrip, get in the cockpit with your own gold-plated key, turn it on and even start it down the runway, all by yourself? No, brother, *you'd better get some instruction* —a lot of detailed and comprehensive instruction. And you had better spend some quality time with an experienced instructor before you ever take that plane off the ground. If you don't, you might get it into the air by some freaky luck—but I can almost guarantee you that you'll come crashing down, with precious little time to figure out why or even to regret your idiocy. In just that way, the papers are filled with the stories of men who had a good idea, who began businesses and investment opportunities and enterprises, got them off the ground and into operation and apparently were flying high—and then ran into unexpected turbulence that they couldn't handle, and came crashing down in defeat. I won't mention names, but I'm sure you can think of quite a few. And that's what we're trying to avoid, isn't it?

My extremely successful business friend, George Otis, has often said, "I like to work with a Partner who knows tomorrow!" George has spent a lot of time in the book of Proverbs, as well as the rest of the Bible, and he can tell you the same thing that countless other astute businessmen echo: that thirty-one-chapter book, a collection of proverbs put together by King Solomon, is the most practical guide to successful business ever written. I won't say anything further; check it out for yourself. But those truths wouldn't be in the Bible if God didn't *want* you to succeed! He just cares enough about you that He wants to tell you how it works, what pitfalls to avoid, which practices to shun and which to cultivate, in order to succeed. You can't read through the book of Proverbs without knowing that it's *God's* will for you to be successful and prosperous and widely respected, and He tells you *how* to and He also teaches about the rewards of generosity, morality and wisdom. Does that sound bad?

I know one thing; I wish I'd read the first couple of verses of Proverbs 6 a long time ago. "Son, if you endorse a note for someone you hardly know, guaranteeing his debt, you are in serious trouble. You may have trapped yourself by your agreement. Quick! Get out of it if you possibly can! Swallow your pride; don't let embarrassment stand in your way. Go and beg to have your name erased. Don't put it off. Do it now. Don't rest until you do it. If you can get out of this trap you have saved yourself like a deer that escapes from a hunter, or a bird from the net." (Living Bible) If I'd read that years ago—if I had *known* the will of God in matters like that—I would have prayed for a great many of my friends and acquaintances, and tried to help them in some different way than cosigning or guaranteeing their notes. As I look back now, having done it a lot of times, I feel that I very rarely helped anybody; I usually only aggravated a serious problem and put off just briefly a showdown that involved more than the dollars in the loan. There were lessons that these people needed to learn, and my efforts at "helping" only muddied the water. And I wound up paying a lot of those loans off myself!

"Okay, maybe you've got a point, maybe it is *good* to read the Bible and know all that stuff," you may be saying. "But I've got problems *now!* I'm right in the middle of a business crisis, or an urgent family problem, and I don't have time to read the whole Bible. How in the world do *I* get in tune with God's will, so that my prayers can be successful and on target *now?*"

I hear what you're saying, friend, and I understand and sympathize. I wish I could give you a magic key that would instantly clue you to the solution of the problem you're facing currently, but I'm not sure I can. There aren't always shortcuts when we'd like to have them, in flying or business or in prayer. I've been in a lot of emergency situations where I didn't know the will of God, and therefore didn't really know how to pray successfully. I've suffered some business flops and some personal failures and missed out on a lot of wonderful opportunities—simply because I hadn't availed myself of the wisdom to pull it all together and keep it on track. You may lose a couple of battles while you're learning what God's will is, just as I have, but you'll *win the war*, and accomplish your long-range goals, if you'll make a quality commitment *now* to start digging in that Biblical gold mine.

I can offer you three suggestions that *may* help you right now, though. I have to hedge my bets a little bit, because the only *sure* way to success is the way I've outlined already; but each of these temporary methods has helped me squeak through some tough spots.

1. Get with other people, preferably more experienced and knowledgeable believers, and seek God's will in your situation, and pray together about it. I'll devote the next chapter to this theme.

2. Pray right now that God will *direct you* to the passage of Scripture in His Word that speaks specifically to your current need. Many times He'll do just that! Just one very recent example: about a week ago, Shirley and I were agonizing over whether to drop what we were doing and fly to the Bonneville salt flats in Utah to watch our friend Stan Barrett attempt to set a new land speed

94

record. We were buried under our own activities, and very reluctant to fly up there and possibly witness some kind of disaster. We love Stan and Penny and their kids so much, and wanted to support them in prayer, but weren't sure we could or should fly up there to be on the spot. We really didn't know what God's will was in that specific situation, so Shirley did what I'm suggesting. She prayed earnestly for the Lord to show us what His will was, and then she opened her Bible, looking for the word "chariot," which had impressed itself on her mind as she thought about Stan and that thirty-nine-foot rocket car. She checked her concordance, found the word chariot listed several places, but among them in the 8th chapter of the book of Acts. She quickly looked it up, and out of her King James Bible jumped this phrase, as if it were in blazing neon: "Go and join thyself to this chariot"!

We flew up the next day, and were there to pray with Stan and Penny for the successful accomplishment of their incredible goal. At 7:15 on Sunday morning the 9th of September, Stan Barrett guided that chariot over the salt flats at a speed of 638 miles per hour, the fastest man has ever gone on land!

I'm not necessarily advising that you should just open your Bible and read whatever your finger points to, and then let that be your immediate guide. Sometimes this works, even spectacularly. I could give you a lot more examples in my life where it has. But it's not infallible, and it's more of a stopgap or emergency measure; God really wants us to be mature sons and daughters, and really know how to pray in any specific situation, according to His will.

3. Get out by yourself, set aside some quiet time, ask God what you want to—and then sit and listen for what He may tell you. As we've already discussed, God is Spirit, and *you* are Spirit at your inner core, and He really

wants to develop a conversational relationship with you on that level. But that takes time and quiet—and both those commodities are in short supply these days. You have to practically carve them out, and that takes commitment. I'm talking about anything from half an hour to a week at a time. If you're really looking for specific answers, and you just don't have any idea of what God's will would be in that situation, tell Him that honestly. Sit quietly or walk along a country road, and ask Him, just as the disciples did of Jesus, to teach you how to pray effectively. Mull the situation or the person that you're praying about over and over in your mind, asking God to show you the truth of the specific situation, from His omniscient viewpoint. Ask Him to show you what His will is, and perhaps you'll visualize it—perhaps you'll just come to a quiet *knowing* of how to proceed—or perhaps you'll discover your own motives and see the problem or the person in a totally different light. This is what honest prayer often does. It helps you to see a person or situation as it really *is*, and not necessarily the way you'd like it to be. Like the teenage kid who wants the car before he's old enough, to accomplish his immediate goal might be to jeopardize his whole life.

The Bible actually says that "and in the same way—by our faith—the Holy Spirit helps us with our daily problems and with our praying. But we don't even know what we should pray for, nor how to pray as we should; but the Holy Spirit (God's own Spirit/Person) *prays for us* with such feeling that it cannot be expressed in words. And the Father who knows all hearts, knows, of course, what the Spirit is saying as He pleads for us in harmony with God's own will. And we know that all that happens to us is working for our good if we love God and are fitting into His plans." (Romans 8:26–28) (Living Bible)

Isn't that comforting? Isn't it good to know that, if you're really honest and sincere in wanting to pray according to God's will, that He'll personally help you as you grope for the right way to pray? Isn't that just like a loving Father? He knows that this language is difficult for us, and that the whole world system puts it down, telling us that it's child's play and superstition or totally irrelevant. He knows we don't have much skill in it, and that it's a system of guidance that we have to learn according to a set of rules that the world knows little about—and so He offers us His own supernatural help. But we have to care enough, on our end of the thing, to take some time and be quiet enough to hear His gentlemanly voice. You see, in many ways we've got to change, if we want to accomplish our goals. Like Eliza Doolittle in *My Fair Lady* it usually requires a transformation of personality and habits for a person to move up from one echelon to another. A great athlete has to develop discipline and character; the top businessman has to develop perseverance and judgment and dependability; the political leader has to relinquish some of his short-term pleasures to develop habits and procedures that will accomplish his long-range objectives. And so there's no point in trying to "con" God, or wheedle Him out of some selfish thing that you'd like to have, if it's not in harmony with His wise and loving will for you. He's been around too long to fall for our attempts at the old soft sell.

Art Robertson of King's College says it well: "The purpose of prayer for the believer is to join with God in what He is doing. God doesn't change, but we do. And when we change, He can work with us in ways that otherwise wouldn't be possible. So I see myself as changing in prayer, as becoming God's instrument through the prayer."

So I suggest this kind of honesty: "Lord, how do I get

from here to there? Will You show me how to accomplish my objectives, to win this goal, to work my way up through the competition and get where I'd like to be? Will You teach me, through a study of Your Word, and by speaking to my spirit inside me, what the realities of the situation are? If I have to wait awhile and learn some more, I'll try to do it gracefully. I don't want to hurt anybody in the process, least of all myself and my family, so I know that I need Your wisdom and guidance.

"I'm beginning to believe that I can count on You. I understand that Jesus made this conversation possible, that He has already paid for it, so I'll just thank You in advance—in His name."

Then stop, look and listen—and get ready for results!

In everything you do, put God first, and He will direct you and crown your efforts with success. (Proverbs 3:6, LB)

8 The Multiple Effect

Well, we've talked about some pretty heavy things, haven't we?

And so far, almost everything I've said has placed the responsibility and the initiative in your court. Prayer *is* largely a private thing, between an individual and God. It usually involves individual concerns, and should involve an individual approach.

But it doesn't have to always be a solo effort.

Why would Donald Seibert, Chairman of the J. C. Penney Company, meet with William Kanaga, the Chairman of Arthur Young & Company and Howard Kauffmann, President of the Exxon Corporation, *once a week at 7:00 A.M.?* Are they meeting to effect some unlikely merger between the giant retailer and the massive oil company, with one of the nation's largest accounting firms engineering the deal? What has either of these companies got to do with the others? And what's so urgent that they have to meet behind closed doors—so early that most corporate executives haven't nibbled their first soft-boiled eggs yet?

It's urgent business, all right: they meet to study the Bible together! And they *do* effect a merger: they join together in mutual prayer. It's important enough to these men that they try to meet once a week, for at least an hour. In a recent *Christian Herald* interview, Donald Seibert revealed, "we proceed very slowly because we'll get on one question that will remind somebody of something that happened to him and presented a problem, and then we'll talk about that for the rest of the hour. We share personal concerns with one another, and it's tremendously helpful."

Would you say that these men should probably have a pretty good grasp of reality, of priorities and time/cost effectiveness? With all the other activities that could occupy their time and thoughts, do you think these men would go to such lengths *unless* there was a positive and practical benefit? The answer is obvious.

The Governor of Minnesota, Al Quie, and former Iowa Senator Harold Hughes are mainstays of another weekly prayer/strategy group that includes evangelist Doug Coe and former presidential aide Chuck Colson. There was a time, not very long ago really, when some of these men literally couldn't stand each other—they were poles apart ideologically and politically—but now they eagerly meet to pray and help each other in whatever they can. Although they are not able to meet as regularly as they'd like, because of their divergent geographical commitments, they've found their sessions to be an invaluable part of their spiritual growth. The format for their group is similar to that used by the New York businessmen. During the hour and a half they're together, they devote about a half hour to Bible study, a half hour or more to sharing their problems and needs, and then ten or fifteen minutes at the end to praying in accordance with God's will as they've discovered it during their sessions.

And meetings like this are going on in hundreds, perhaps thousands of places throughout the country every week! The Full Gospel Businessmen's group, for example, meets in at least a couple of hundred locations every Saturday morning around 7:00 a.m.—and the average attendance at these breakfast-prayer sessions numbers in the hundreds! These meetings include business and professional people from every walk of life and economic level. I've attended several of the Presidential Prayer Breakfasts in Washington, D.C., and have been absolutely astounded at the high level of attendance and interest on the part of international leaders in the world of business and politics. Now these breakfasts are growing in popularity across the country, in many states, and cities.

Why? What's this activity all about? Very simply, *there is a dynamic in group prayer that often transcends individual and separate ones.*

James, the half-brother of Jesus, wrote in his epistle, "The prayer of a righteous man has great power in its effects." (James 5:16, RSV). And that's true! But when you get two or more righteous men or women *together* in prayer, a kind of "multiple effect" seems to come into play. Quite often, group prayer releases a special kind of spiritual power—a power that can greatly enhance the benefits you receive from your private communications with God.

Jesus Himself underscored this multiple effect in group prayer when He told His disciples in Matthew 18:19–20 that He would always be in the midst of them *when two or three were gathered in His name.* And He said, "if two of you agree on earth about anything you ask, it will be done for you by My Father in heaven." As a matter of fact, I believe that the cumulative effects of two righteous, God-fearing people praying together can be considerably greater than the results if the two of them pray indvidually and alone.

But why should this be so? Because it's a spiritual principle, and prayer is a spiritual activity—*often against spiritual opposition in an unseen, spiritual dimension.* Remember, prayer doesn't operate according to any natural law; it's an excursion into a vast and invisible realm where blind faith is the key to success and the "buddy" system is a very good idea. Early in the Bible, in Deuteronomy 32:30, the venerable Moses says that one person chased a thousand people—but then *two* "put ten thousand to flight." With God helping then, two people had ten times the effect that one did! President Johnson used to quote the following Scripture which asks, "how can two men walk together unless they be agreed?" There is power in agreement! (Amos 3:3)

That's true in sports, politics, in business, in almost every human activity. It's on that basis that President Carter asked Prime Minister Begin and President Sadat to meet him at Camp David. He hoped to bring about an agreement, in principle and spirit, that in turn would make possible accord on all the practical issues of peace in the Middle East. Each of these men quoted the Bible and the Koran and asked for the prayers of believing people everywhere that they might be *agreed* in their efforts.

Between you and me, I think the main reason that God *requires* that we meet and pray together is that He really doesn't want to encourage maverick spirituality. He really wants us to need and appreciate each other, and so He promises to pay special attention to prayers of agreement between two or more of His children. Strangely enough, though, there's a streak in human nature that rebels against this idea. Most of us don't *want* to depend on somebody else, especially someone that we might consider personally inferior to us. So lots of guys say, "I don't go to church or like to get together with other Christians—because so many of them are hypocrites." You've heard that, haven't you? Surely you haven't said it yourself? But this *is* one of the hundreds of reasons people use to rationalize their failure to pray and worship together. God just doesn't buy that; if people really are hypocrites, then they *need* to be in church, where they get changed! And He might just want to use *you* as an instrument to bring about that change! We've all got blind spots, and perhaps even a hypocrite can help you locate yours.

But fault finding and fault correcting are not the main objectives of group prayer sessions. No, I think God designed marriage for that. All kinds of folks are discovering the practical side of group sessions—therapy sessions, EST, marriage encounter retreats, Esalen, Alcoholics Anonymous, bridge parties, poker games—even hot tubs! I'm not recommending all these things, understand, but they *are* evidence that people have learned they can discover things about themselves and their social environment by "laying it all on the table" and "telling it like it is," voluntarily peeling off some of their protective outer covering so that others can help them solve their own personal riddles. There's embarrassment in many of these methods, shame and pain and revelation; but quite often, I'm told, there are real discoveries and very helpful perceptions, as well.

So—if there's good in some of these *human* methods, why not go right to the top of the class? Why not look for a meeting *where God Himself is one of the participants*, willing to help you diagnose your problems and find the solutions? Doesn't that sound infinitely better? You see, in most small prayer groups members share some of their most vital concerns with each other, in depth, and consider them in the light of the Scripture. One may have discovered a relevant Scripture that the others don't know about, and one may have had a similar experience in which God showed him the answer. When they get around to offering a specific prayer, it's usually with a more certain sense of just *how* to pray, in accordance with God's will about that problem. The Bible promises us that the Lord Himself, by His Spirit, will be present and active in meetings like this, guiding the participants into a deeper understanding about what His will is and how to approach the problems successfully. He uses the interaction to weave them together into a spiritual family. Unless you've been part of something like this, you can't comprehend the surprising love that can begin to animate widely different kinds of people, and cause them to really care about each other. In this day of alienation and estrangement and loneliness, these meetings can be truly wonderful.

Here's an example of what I'm talking about: One of the many small prayer groups that meet in New York City involves five businessmen who meet in midtown Manhattan. These are practical guys who get together to discuss and pray about their real nitty-gritty problems. One of the fellas is a self-employed management consultant named Mike. Not long ago, he was really sweating over his financial situation and his seeming inability to gain complete control over his money and material resources. And he's supposed to be a management expert! As the group discussed his situation with him, one of the others asked a surprising question: "Mike, are you tithing?"

"Tithing! You mean giving away a tenth of everything I make? Man, I'm not making ends meet with a *hundred* percent—I'd do even worse with ninety! Besides, I just don't understand that whole idea; what does God need with my money? Didn't Jesus say we'd always have the poor with us anyway?"

Suddenly it was clear to the rest of the group that they'd found Mike's "blind spot," the very area that God wanted to deal with in Mike's life. Through the discussion, there surfaced a number of passages from the Bible, including Malachi 3:10, Luke 6:38, and 2 Corinthians 9:6–7, all of which make it clear that God wants to get in "a giving contest" with us! He challenges us to try and outgive Him—and there's no way you can win! In each of these Scriptures He promises to heap material blessings on us, faster than we can give them away, if we'll just start the ball rolling ourselves. It's another act of faith—but once you get started, you'll never stop. Or want to!

Finally one of the group observed, "It seems to me, Mike, that you've got your priorities turned around."

"What do you mean?" Mike answered.

"I mean you're putting the cart before the horse; you feel you don't have quite enough money or the proper management of what you have, so you're trying to figure out a way to stretch it further or to make more. Maybe later you'd consider giving some of it away. What you really need to do is start giving it to the Lord right now, so that He can multiply it back to you."

Mike mulled that over for a while and grinned sheepishly. He admitted that with all his concern about finances, his business was not going well at all. It had been months since a substantial contract had come through for him, and he was even beginning to wonder whether he would have to abandon his business altogether. Something inside him told him that his friends were right, that he'd heard from the Lord through them, in their intimate little circle. He began to get a little excited about it, because he'd learned that he could trust God, and now he had a sense of what the Lord really wanted him to do. So he did it! Right then and there, in that meeting, he decided to turn his financial situations completely over to God, and he and his friends had an enthusiastic and specific prayer about it. While he was praying, Mike resolved to give at least a tenth of all his earnings from that time on, and even felt eager to do it. As the meeting broke up, he left with a strange confidence that things were about to change dramatically and that God would respond to his prayer in keeping with His promises, like the one in 2 Corinthians 9:6 "He who sows bountifully will also reap bountifully."

Mike sowed—and then reaped bountifully. Before the end of the year he had obtained *four major new business contracts*, and stepped up his giving considerably. He'd still have to go some to catch up with Art DeMoss, who founded his National Liberty Insurance Company with the resolve to give God ninety percent or more of his annual income—and he did extremely well keeping what was left over!

There's no set format for these prayer sessions around the country. But almost all of them involve considerable discussion about real problems, family lives, job needs and personal conflicts, lots of Bible reading and plenty of specific prayer. People get involved with each other— and the Lord gets involved with all of them!

I'm a group prayer person myself; I have to be. I travel so much that I feel a strong need to latch on to praying people wherever I find them, almost like a drinking man looks for a bar. I'm fortunate to be an elder at The Church on the Way in Van Nuys, California. The congregation is so big (over 8,000 members now) that we feel a need, in every service, to stand up and separate into small groups of three to five people and pray with each other for our specific needs. Oh, the whole congregation prays together about a lot of things, on a local and national and global scale, but the only way we can cope with the thousands of individual problems that have been brought to each service is to break up into these little groups. During that part of the service, we'll spend five or ten minutes getting to know each other and voicing our individual concerns and then praying together about them. Again, it might make you feel uncomfortable to imagine yourself in one of these groups—but don't knock it until you've been there. Countless miracles occur in our lives because we come out of our shells and actually get direct and specific with each other and with the Lord.

When I'm on the road, I can't always get to church on a Sunday morning. Either the plane schedules or late nights or lack of familiarity with any of the local churches might rule out that possibility. So, in addition to the home situations I might get invited to during the week, Sunday morning will often find me with my musicians and road manager and whoever else wants to join in, having our own worship service in my hotel room. It's always informal, but we deal with our real life situations and discuss them in the light of Scripture and then pray together. A number of other entertainers are starting to do the same thing.

Yes, there's more than safety in numbers. There can be guidance and growth and exciting answers to prayer! What you get out of these sessions may very well be related to what you put into them. If you're honest and open and really desire to help and be helped, I'd welcome you into my prayer circle anytime. Professor Art Robertson adds, "Some people say categorically that prayer in large groups is more powerful than praying singly, but I think that's a relative thing. For example, the Queen of Scotland said she feared the prayers of John Knox more than the armies of the world—and that was only one man. And I myself believe that one man might be more effectual than a thousand of lesser faith. On the other hand, a thousand John Knoxes would be more powerful in prayer than one John Knox. I think that's true because

God meant for the many Christian individuals to act as one body. No one of us has a corner on God, so we certainly need one another. Paul says in Romans 14:7, RSV: "None of us lives to himself, and none of us dies to himself." There are many different individual gifts in the body of Christ, and God expects us to help one another. When you have a number of people joined together in prayer, it's much easier to see different facets and insights into the same problem—and it's also much easier to ferret out God's will."

By the way, you don't always have to be *asking* God for something to enjoy the experience of prayer, or to benefit from it. Let's take a closer look now at some of the *other* exciting varieties of supernatural communication!

9 Choosing Your Prayer Frequency

Friend, I'm assuming that you're serious now about prayer.

You might have flicked through the pages with some mild interest, or read two or three chapters out of curiosity or a vague sense of need—but if you're with me this far, I figure you're not playing games. You really *want* to develop a rich and varied relationship with the God of heaven and earth, and realize that the language of prayer is an indispensable part of it. From here on, I want you to understand that *every* kind of honest prayer somehow fits in with the accomplishing of your goals, even though you might not be asking for anything specifically.

As a father, I know the feeling of being wheedled or "buttered up" by one of my daughters when she wanted something; and even then it was sometimes irresistible when I knew that she was putting her arms around me and kissing me merely as an overture to asking for something. But my desire to give to my daughters flourished much more in an atmosphere of full, well-rounded, loving relationship than through any girlish tactics.

God's like that. He's the ultimate Father, and all of our better instincts and feelings originated in His heart. We didn't make them up! And I'm telling you, as one of His kids, it's *fun* to know God!

There's no limit to the number of ways that you can communicate with Him. I sometimes imagine a CB radio with no limits on the low or high frequencies. Like most CB radios, heaven has the capacity both to send and receive signals. The Lord has a number of "handles"—Father, Son, Holy Spirit, Jehovah, mighty God, Prince of Peace, Counselor, Lord and a great many others that He reveals in the Bible—and He can be reached on as many frequencies as there are people with prayer transmitters in their own hearts.

I certainly don't intend to be trivial or cute about this, but I want to illustrate that there's a great variety of ways in which the Lord is willing to be approached. He's accessible, and much easier to reach than most of us realize. Someone came up with the acronym "ACTS"—standing for Adoration, Confession, Thanksgiving and Supplication—as an inventory of prayer frequencies; and though I think that each one is valid, I believe the catalog may be much broader.

Still, let's look at these four frequencies, and without subscribing to any prearranged order or ritual, see if you don't agree that you should dial God every day through each of these channels.

Adoration. I like to begin my day by spending some time telling God how I feel about Him. I really love Him! He knows it, but we both feel it's important that I express it in fresh and honest ways. The Lord appreciates it, and it does wonderful things for me, way down deep.

110

In my spiritual autobiography, *A New Song*, I actually borrowed the title and basic theme from the Psalmist David, who many times said, "I will sing a new song unto the Lord, for He has done wonderful things!" (Psalm 98 and others) Many times one of the Psalms says exactly what I want to say; other times I really want to put it in my own words.

I might just say, "Lord, I really *love* You! My love's not perfect; it's often muddy with self-love, but You can read my heart, Lord, and You know I really do love You more than anything else in my life." Sometimes, as I praise and worship God, I flash back to the starry-eyed way I used to look at Shirley before we got married. I can remember when we used to sit next to each other in a high school class, I'd sometimes feel her knee next to mine or maybe briefly touch her hand as we were exchanging papers. Those fleeting encounters would give me a little tingle that can only occur when you're deeply in love with someone. I'm sure you've experienced that kind of thing yourself, and you may not yet feel that you can share feelings like that with God—but I'm just telling you now, as you get to know Him better you'll really be in love with Him.

Let me try to picture it another way. I keep coming back to the love a father has for his children, because that's truly the way God loves us. And I've had the experience, both from the child's perspective and from the parent's. I really treasured the times when my four daughters were little girls. I remember so well the countless times one of them would get out her crayons and paper and scribble on it intently for a few minutes, and then hand it to me with a shy smile.

After studying the wrinkled piece of paper with its unintelligible lines of color for a minute or two, I'd ask, "That's pretty, honey! What does it say?"

"It says, 'I love you,'" she'd answer. And then she'd

hop up on my lap and give me a big hug and kiss. I still have boxes and mounds of these ragged slips of "love letters" from my kids, and I wouldn't dream of throwing them away. For them, those simple messages were statements of adoration and worship—and I think our prayers of adoration to God should capture some of the same simplicity.

Here's another image. I remember reading a cartoon once that showed a small child inside on a rainy day.

"Why is it raining outside?" the little boy asked.

"God's crying." his mother responded.

"Why is He crying?"

"He's sad about things not going right in the world. He's crying for the hungry and sick people."

After thinking about that for a minute or so, the little boy drew some pictures with happy faces and told his mother, "Now, I'm going to make God smile." Then he held the pictures up to the window, facing the sky—and it immediately stopped raining. I love that.

Believe me, He loves to receive our praise and worship and expressions of satisfaction about just being in His presence. A lot of religion is just pompous ritual, and God really doesn't need that from us, does He? After all, Einstein and Schweitzer were just babies in His sight, intellectually and philosophically. Jesus actually urges us to be more like children in our response to God. And often, the more childlike and unsophisticated we can become during these periods of adoration, the more likely we are to please God and get ourselves into a spiritually sensitive mood that will help us discern His will as we turn to other prayer frequencies.

Thanksgiving. Praise and thanksgiving often overlap, though giving thanks to God is different from praising Him in that the act of thanking usually arises from something specific God has already done for us. It's hard to draw a line, though, because when you're thinking about all the good things the Lord may have done for you, or for your family or your friends, or in your business, it's hard not to let recognition of who He is (praise) filter into the thanksgiving process—things like "Praise the Lord!" or "That's wonderful, Father, and so are You!" And believe me, that's perfectly okay.

I often just thank God spontaneously when I notice Him doing something for me or someone else. When I'm eating in a crowded restaurant, for example, I'll remember God regularly gives me and my family enough to eat, so, rather than offering a long-winded prayer that might attract undue attention, I'll just raise my eyes to heaven and say, "Thanks, Lord!"

No big deal; He knows I mean it and He gets the message.

But it's too easy for many Americans to take their blessings for granted, so I would also advise setting aside regular times during the week when you do nothing but offer thanks to God for all He's done for you. That time of thanksgiving might be during your regular morning prayer time, or at a family supper, or perhaps at a special time you set aside later in the evening.

One couple I know decided they didn't devote enough time to thanking God, so they made it a point to kneel down together just before bedtime to pray *only* prayers of thanks. They found it was difficult not to slip in a little request now and then—but mainly they just brought up blessing after blessing, running over an ever-expanding list of ways the Lord had showed His love for them; sometimes, they'd end up weeping for pure joy.

There's real power in that! A lot of people don't realize how rich they are; Irving Berlin wrote a fine song called "Count Your Blessings," and if we all did that regularly, we'd have a much stronger sense of self-worth and of the loving provision of God. And, though it may be early to introduce this concept right now, our eventual goal in thanksgiving is to "give thanks in all circumstances." (1 Thessalonians 5:18, RSV) Eventually you'll learn to perceive God working in *every* event in your life, even if the immediate impact seems bad, and get into the habit of thanking Him in advance for working everything out in your best interests.

I don't mean that you'll become a hopeless Pollyanna; you'll still be living in a real world, but experience in trusting God does develop confidence, which leads to thanksgiving even when things look bleak. You *know* you'll be coming out on top!

Confession. Do I detect a shudder, a slight wincing at this subject? Well, don't draw back—it'll do ya good!

Once in a while I'll meet someone who says something like, "What is guilt, anyway? I've never felt guilt in my life! I've always tried to do the right thing, and have never had any pangs of conscience or anything like that."

That kind of person is very rare; in fact, it's such an exception in today's world that I hardly know how to explain it. Because most people truly do feel guilty. Most people are quite aware of the kinds of things they've done in their lives that they wish they could go back and undo, and they certainly *do* feel riddled with guilt and shame in their consciences.

Guilt is a crippler. There are more people in the hospitals and on the psychiatrists' couches right now because of guilt and anxiety than for any other root cause. The noted psychologist Dr. Karl Menninger recently wrote a big best-selling book called *Whatever Happened to Sin?* about man's psychological need for forgiveness. It was a startling book, because most of the psychiatric community downgrades religion and the Biblical ideas of sin and atonement and forgiveness. But Dr. Menninger faced the problem squarely, realizing that people *do* feel guilty, their consciences *are* wormy and stained, and that it's not enough simply to help a patient understand *why* he feels that way. He really needs to be forgiven! He needs to be cleansed!

I've told the story before about the mousy patient who took up so much of her psychiatrist's time. One day, at his own wits' end, he leveled with her: "Let's face it, Mrs. Jones. You don't have an inferiority complex—you *are* inferior!" And Dr. Menninger says to us, loud and clear, "Guilt complex? Forget about the 'complex'—we *are* guilty!"

Much more typical in today's permissive society is the reaction of a young Jewish girl, one of my daughter's best friends: "My parents don't really care what I do. They've never given me many rules, and even when I broke them it didn't seem to matter very much. They don't make me feel that anything I do is necessarily wrong—so why in the world do I feel guilty?"

The answer is simple. The Bible tells us that God has written His law into every man's heart—a certain amount of it is programmed into us—and as moral beings, we *know* that it's wrong to be dishonest, to be completely selfish, to hurt other people needlessly, to be sexually promiscuous, to stand in the way of another person's good. We know it! Nobody has to tell us, though one person's conscience may be more highly educated than another's. From the time we're infants, we begin to store up little stains and scars and little invisible canker sores of guilt, and these things begin to gnaw at us subconsciously, accusing us and creating anxieties and tensions and unexplainable dissatisfactions. Quite often they make us feel unworthy of our own goals and aspirations, and we really don't feel we deserve to win. Physical illnesses grow out of these feelings, and all kinds of warped lives.

Are you getting the picture?

We could go into this in much greater detail, but we

won't. Please just accept that you *need* to confess your own wrongdoings to somebody, and to be forgiven, for your own sake—physically and emotionally, as well as spiritually. And God is the One we need to make our confessions to. The Bible, in 1 John 1:9 says, "If we confess our sins, He is faithful and just, *and will forgive our sins and cleanse us from all unrighteousness.*" (RSV) There is, in fact, nowhere else to go for ultimate forgiveness! That's what Jesus' death on the cross was all about; since God created us in His image, and since our willful disobedience separates every one of us from Him, Jesus paid the ultimate price to make possible a reconciliation and a complete cleansing, taking our guilt and the consequences of it on Himself. But each of us has to avail himself of that cleansing individually, by trading in our separate selfish acts and sins for His *righteousness.* It's free—but it's not automatic.

So spend some time in prayer, both asking for general forgiveness and cleansing, and being *specific* about individual acts that you want to be washed away and corrected. As you learn more about God's Word and His provision for you, you'll begin to experience the exhilarating feeling of being truly forgiven and cleansed of the cancerous infection called sin. And as that happens—new power will begin to permeate your prayers.

Supplication. Supplication is asking God for things. And asking and asking and asking. I'm not talking about begging, really, but rather a consistent and committed kind of asking—the kind that intends to get results. We've talked in some detail about asking but it *is* one of the important "prayer frequencies," and there's an aspect we haven't really touched on much.

Most of us tend to get so wrapped up in our own problems and concerns that we pray primarily for ourselves—our own finances, careers, popularity and other involvements—and we pray for others mostly as an afterthought. God, though, wants us to pray about the details in the lives of others as well as ourselves.

And He even wants us to pray for our enemies!

Insurance magnate Arthur DeMoss, relying on such passages as Matthew 5:44, RSV, where Jesus says, "Love your enemies and *pray for those who persecute you*," made it a practice to pray for enemies over the years. And the results have been striking, to say the least.

On one occasion, for example, an executive who worked for him at the National Liberty Mutual Company had to be fired, and it fell to Art to handle the termination. "I tried to handle the matter as humanely as possible," he recalled. "Both of us agreed the thing wasn't working, and when he asked for what I thought was excessive termination pay, I nevertheless agreed to it. But after the man left us, a year went by and he didn't get another job. I could understand his getting discouraged, but then he and his wife got bitter and critical toward me and our company."

The man began "backbiting with others in the company and began advising people who were considering coming to work for us to stay away," DeMoss said. "But I started praying for him—just that the Lord would bless him—and soon he got another job and wound up apologizing to me. As a matter of fact, we became good friends after that."

Rather amazing behavior for a top corporate executive, wouldn't you say?

Art also encountered hostility from people *outside* his company, and once again prayer played an integral part in helping him keep perspective and also in resolving the situation. "We've had an inordinate success in building a good-sized business, and that's bound to attract some criticism," he said. "Not everyone rejoices with you when you do well, but one way or another prayer always provides some answers. There's no promise, of course,

117

that the 'enemies' you're praying for will become any less hostile. For example, one of our critics a few years ago was an insurance commissioner from one of the Southern states. These guys have the power of life and death over you, and he came out and publicly assailed us in the press for what he charged were improper business practices on our part. We could have sued him, but it's like fighting Tammany Hall."

For National Liberty Mutual, this was "a costly experience in terms of loss of public confidence," Art told me. "We use Art Linkletter in our advertising, and they accused him of selling insurance without a license—but that's ridiculous, because he's *endorsing* our insurance, not selling it! The commissioner could have attacked me and nobody would have paid much attention, but when he attacked Linkletter, it made headlines in the newspapers. So I started praying for this guy. I never prayed for anything bad to happen to him—but *he wound up getting put out of office and being indicted.*"

Draw your own conclusions.

DeMoss' business continued to prosper, so his critics have had little lasting effect on him. But it would be interesting to speculate what might have happened if he had failed to "pray for his enemies." It's important to emphasize, by the way, that he *didn't* pray that God would strike down these critics, but just that He would bless them. The Christian way is to show love to our enemies and to leave vengeance, if vengeance is appropriate at all, in God's hands. I know, from my own bitter experience, that God has sometimes "blessed me" by letting me fall on my face; I've learned some of my most valuable lessons from my failures. So it's not necessarily "vengeance" when God "blesses" you by pulling the rug out from under you—or your enemy.

I know this idea of praying for your enemies and then waiting for God to act in some way you may not even expect is a hard pill to swallow, and I myself have sometimes balked at asking God to bless those who have used me wrongly. But the more you try this approach in your prayers of supplication, the more confidence you'll get in leaving not only yourself and your friends—but your adversaries as well—in God's hands.

There are many other kinds of prayers of supplication, such as those for healing, for political leaders and for financial crises, but those will be dealt with in other contexts. For now, just remember that God wants you to ask Him for *whatever* you feel you or others really need. No item is too small, no request too insignificant. He wants to hear from you, and one way or another, He'll respond as your loving Father.

Some people, when they first begin to pray (and occasionally long after), recite beautifully worded written prayers that say just what they want to express. They may graduate to writing their own, carefully choosing words that convey their thoughts, feelings and needs. And that's fine if they're really sincere.

But this should be only temporary, or an *addition* to spontaneous expression. After a while, "ready made" should become "ready prayed," so much a part of you that you don't have to remember them consciously any more. They just come out naturally in your own words.

Consider "The Lord's Prayer" as exhibit A.

Jesus offered this prayer in Matthew 6:9–13 and Luke 11:2–4, in response to His own disciples' request, "Lord, teach us to pray." The short example that He gave is so power-packed so eminently all-inclusive in its general scope, that it's the most perfect prayer ever uttered. Whole or substantial portions of books, many of them, have been written on this one prayer. A couple of best ones are C. S. Lewis' *Letters to Malcolm: Chiefly on Prayer* and W. Phillip Keller's *A Layman Looks at the Lord's Prayer*. Obviously, then, this is not the place to go into much detail—but let's take a very brief look at each phrase, as a spur to your own thinking.

"Our Father who art in heaven" ... When Jesus uttered these words, they were revolutionary. People just weren't used to thinking of God as Father! Something in that word speaks to us of warm, intimate, personal relationship, and that's exactly what Jesus intended to convey. Regardless of our age, each of us should approach a loving Father/God as His child, believing that He wants our ultimate good. God *does* rule in heaven, which is not just a place but an eternal spiritual dimension—and still He is also present with us through His Personal Presence, the Holy Spirit. So the prayer begins like a call to the Head Office, where the Chairman of the Board happens to be our Father!

"Hallowed be thy name" ... When Moses asked for the name of the One who spoke to him from the burning bush and commissioned him to demand the Israelites' freedom from Pharaoh, God answered, *"I am."*

Think of it. His very name describes omnipotence, eternal power and supreme knowledge. Although He offers us His divine hand in partnership, He is indescribably superior to us and is worthy of our most reverent worship. These are words of *praise*—one of your major "prayer frequencies."

"Thy kingdom come" ... God's Kingdom has a two-fold existence—both within *you* in the immediate present if you're committed to Him, and in the world at large. I sometimes substitute one word, and say, "Thy kingdom advance...," because it implies a deepening and broadening sphere of influence, both in me and in the world around me. When an explorer plants his country's flag on the shore of a new territory, he claims that whole territory for his sovereign—but there may be many a skirmish and a lot of blood, sweat and tears

before that territory truly becomes part of the "kingdom."

God's kingdom *is* advancing, relentlessly, even through this discussion that you and I are having.

"Thy will be done, on earth as it is in heaven" . . . To be completely in tune with God, or in real communication with Him, it's necessary for you to accept or submit to His will as you perceive it, even though that divine will may not seem too palatable at first. I'm reminded of a journalist friend who felt God prodding him to join an evangelistic mission to Northern Ireland. He wasn't particularly interested in going because he had other responsibilities at home—and besides, those reports of terrorist bombs in Belfast didn't appeal to him at all! But after a considerable amount of prayer and Bible reading, he decided to go, and the trip turned into one of the spiritual highlights of his life. He learned to trust God in a physically dangerous environment and also made friends with whom he has maintained close ties to this day. In some cases, God may just want you to accept passively what He has willed, and learn to trust that He's orchestrating everything for your own good. In other cases, as with my journalist friend, He may want you to become an active instrument in *accomplishing* His will. In any and all cases, the ultimate demonstration of confidence in our Father is to say, "I trust You, Lord. Let's do it Your way."

"Give us this day our daily bread" . . . This is an exciting part of this prayer!

God really cares about our material needs, really wants our bills to get paid and for there to be healthy food on our tables! Lots of things have to happen to bring that about—and none of them are beyond His control. You're not likely to walk into the breakfast nook, snap your finger and expect a loaf of bread to materialize on the table; it *could* happen, but it's not likely. Instead, for you and your family to have what you really need, your job will have to go well, the economy will have to survive, the truck strike will have to be settled, the crops will have to get enough rain—all kinds of things.

But Jesus says don't worry about it—God's got it under control! As a booster shot to your faith on this point, read Matthew 6:25–34.

"And forgive us our debts, as we also have forgiven our debtors" ... We've talked about this forgiveness principle already. Let me underscore it again: unless you're willing to truly forgive, and *be* forgiven, the effectiveness of your prayers will be severely limited. "Our debts" are our sins, our selfish and hurtful acts and thoughts, and we should get specific about them and deal with them separately—as you usually do with your other debts. Very significantly, the way Jesus phrases this principle, we're evidently expected to have already wiped out the debts of others, before our own are marked PAID IN FULL.

"And lead us not into temptation, but deliver us from evil" ... "Temptation" may sound like an old-fashioned religious word, but you know what it means. It means the very strong desire to do something that's wrong, that has a moral or spiritual price tag beyond your ability to pay it. It would most certainly lead to a "debt," a sin. So why should Jesus pray that God won't *"lead* us" into temptation?

Let's check the Word again. We know from James 1:13–15 that God doesn't tempt anybody—it's our own passions and the devil himself who do that. What Jesus seems to be requesting here is that God protect us from circumstances that may lead us to succumb to temptation. He's saying, "Lord, don't allow us through our own weaknesses to fall into a moral or spiritual trap which enables Satan, the 'evil' or 'evil one' in this prayer, to triumph over us." Or as the Apostle Paul puts it: "No temptation has overtaken you that is not common to man. God is faithful, and he will not let you be tempted beyond your strength, but *with the temptation will also provide the way of escape*, that you may be able to endure it." (1 Corinthians 10:13, RSV)

It's almost like "Thy will be done" again—but God wants you to voice your *own* will in this matter, to agree with Him for your benefit. Do you understand what I'm saying?

"For thine is the kingdom and the power and the glory, for ever. Amen" . . . For some reason, some Bible translations don't include this phrase, but it has become a standard conclusion for the Lord's Prayer, and I think it belongs. The more you get to know your Father, the more natural it will be to begin and end every prayer with praise and recognition of who He is. Like the childish pride that cries, "My Dad can lick your Dad!", you'll realize that *God's* identity is rubbing off on *you*, saying a great deal about who *you* are.

We've hardly scratched the surface, touching only a few of the "prayer frequencies" available to us. As you become more fluent in your own supernatural language, you'll have lots of incidents and insights to share with *me*. And that's how it should be; I'll be eager to hear them.

In fact, that's what I want to talk about next—listening.

10 How to Listen for Supernatural Answers

At the risk of boring you slightly, let me repeat the story about Oral Roberts and Merv Griffin that I told you earlier.

Oral was a guest on the *Merv Griffin Show*.

Thinking perhaps he might put Oral on the spot or at least get into a provocative subject, Merv asked, "Oral, I hear that you've actually heard God speak to you—is that right?"

Oral paused just a moment, looked at Merv quite directly with a little smile, and answered softly, "Merv, —God's spoken to *you* many times, too—haven't you heard Him?"

People aren't very good at listening these days. Oh, we're great at talking—there's a regular cacophony of dialogue going on all the time. But *listening* is another matter. It's almost a lost art. And I'm just as guilty as anybody; often at parties or other kinds of social gatherings, I catch myself forming my own sentences mentally while watching somebody else's mouth move, and never really hear what they're saying. Even their names go right in one ear and out the other.

It's really a selfish, egocentric kind of thing. Most of us feel the world revolves around us, and are in love with the sound of our own voices and ideas. It's no wonder, then, that we're not very good at praying—because effective praying involves listening for God's answers.

Remember the "Galloping Gourmet," Graham Kerr? Well, he tells this story about himself. Over a period of some years, he and his wife, Treena, developed one of the most successful shows in the history of international television, a widely popular cooking show. Then he had a dramatic encounter with Jesus, and became just as enthusiastic about his new Christian life as he'd been about his cooking and his TV career. He was quite proud of the amount of time he was devoting to prayer each day, including talking to God in the shower! But when he mentioned his prayer life to a more mature believer, the man responded, "And how much do you listen?"

It took Graham a moment or so to figure out what the fellow was getting at, but then he realized the guy was asking how well he listened for God's *answers*. Graham was just a little flustered, but he finally indicated in a vague way that somehow the answers to prayer seem to come along eventually. He didn't mind waiting; prayer was the thing.

But his companion pressed, "Why do you think there is a delay? Why don't you listen for an answer straight away?"

The idea made sense, and Graham felt he was learning something valuable. He still prays while he is in the shower—but now he listens for an answer while he shaves! And his dramatically transformed life indicates that he gets wonderful answers.*

* For a fuller account of this incident, see William Proctor's *On the Trail of God* (Doubleday: New York City, 1977), p. 24.

Of course God doesn't always answer immediately. We know from Hebrews 6:12 that it often takes patience as well as faith to "inherit the promises" God makes to us. As a matter of fact, it took Abraham over twenty years to receive one of the greatest promises of his life—his son Isaac. But God *may* respond right away, so we'd better keep an ear cocked for His voice in our lives.

A friend of mine named Joy Dawson has more or less specialized in listening to God, and she frequently teaches others how to fine-tune their inner spiritual ears so they can hear His voice more clearly. She often gets such spectacular and specific answers to her own prayers, that Shirley and I became intrigued. We asked her to come to our home one day and share with us some of the secrets that work so well in her own prayer life.

She told us that when she starts to pray, she first says, "Lord, I want to hear from You and You only." Then she moves ahead with a solid reliance on the Scriptures: "The Bible says, 'Resist the devil and he will flee from you,' (James 4:7, RSV), so now in 'resisting the devil' I'm going to say, 'You leave me alone! Don't jam the frequencies of my prayers! I do not want to hear from you, and I will not hear from you. You can't intrude on my thinking, now flee—get away from me. I want to hear only from God!'"

Then Joy turns directly to God and begins to meet some of the prerequisites of prayer we discussed in a previous chapter. "Now, Lord, I'm bringing everything in subjection before You," she prays. "I want to be cleansed. As Jesus taught us, I want to ask Your forgiveness. I want to get me out of the way, and I want to get the devil out of the way. There's nobody else I want to hear from but You, God. And now that I've made my request, I'm going to wait right here and I'm going to listen. I want to hear from You."

And then she listens—just sits and listens.

You can see that through this process Joy is in a sense "clearing the deck" of her life. She takes pains to still her own mind and to subordinate her own desires and selfishness. In this way, she guards against receiving any counterfeit messages and opens herself to hear only valid responses from God Himself. Then, after she's laid her concerns and needs before God, she'll sit quietly for a long time and wait for His response.

Joy has become so adept at this listening phase of divine communication that people frequently call her up to pray for them and their loved ones, and in some ways this bothers her. She's perfectly willing to pray for others and spends a great deal of time in intercessory prayer; but she cautions her students, "This is not all that God wants for these people. He doesn't want people just coming to Joy Dawson to get their answers. No, He wants to communicate *with each one of us.* And after I've shared with you what I've learned from God, I hope you'll go home and practice praying and listening to God yourself, and not just rely on me."

I hear what Joy's saying, and I've tried her method. Though I have told you I am not very good at listening, I am learning—and I have had some remarkable answers from God when I just sat and listened. But God may respond in a variety of ways, and here are a few:

—*Directed thoughts.* Perhaps the most common way that God will respond to you is by prodding your thinking in one direction or another; or He'll encourage in you a definite inner conviction, usually accompanied by a sense of inner peace that a certain course of action is right.

"Now, wait a minute," you may be protesting, "I don't think I want God invading my mind that way; can He do that? That sounds like some kind of mind control." Well, mentalists have already proven that one person can suggest images in the mind of another, especially if the other person is willing and receptive. And that's the key word: receptive. We're not talking about mind control. If you're truly receptive to a Creator/Father, then certainly He has the ability to form certain images and thoughts in your mind. That's really what you're after, isn't it?

God frequently moved in this way through the mind of Francis of Assisi, and because Francis took time to listen, he found that all sorts of seemingly insurmountable problems often got resolved rather easily. For example, Francis' early ministry had been developing rather successfully and so many followers had gravitated around him that he felt the need to establish a rule of order to regulate the activities of his friars. So he drew up a rather simple code, drawn largely from passages from the Gospels and from manual labor practices he had found to be workable, and went to Rome to have them approved by Pope Innocent III.

Unfortunately, some of the Pope's advisers opposed the formation of this new Franciscan order, which had become quite popular throughout the country, and so the Pope was reluctant to give Francis the green light. Innocent objected that the way of life the Franciscans wanted to lead would be too hard, and none of Francis' arguments seemed powerful enough to move him to a final positive decision. In effect, the Pope just let the matter hang, and Francis was at a loss to know how to get him off dead center.

So with all human efforts exhausted, the merchant's-son-turned-saint began to rely exclusively on the spiritual secret weapon that had sustained him so marvelously in the past—private prayer. He didn't just present his difficulty to God and then rise up from his knees and go about his business, however. Like any effective conversationalist, he said his piece and then became silent and waited for his Companion's response. And the answer wasn't long in coming.

As Francis got deeply immersed in a "conversation with Jesus," a full-blown parable came into his mind. It went like this:

> It seems there was a beautiful but poor woman who lived in a desert land. The king of the land noticed her one day and, taken with her beauty, he wanted to marry her, in part because he knew what attractive children they would have.
>
> So the king and the beauty were wed, and they had many sons; but the king, who was quite busy with his affairs of state, wasn't able to be around as they were growing up. The woman continued to live in the desert, where she raised their sons. When the boys had matured, however, their mother sent them to the king's court, and the king, immediately struck by their good looks, asked, "Whose sons are you?"
>
> After they informed him they were the sons of the poor woman of the desert, the king hugged them and replied, "Have no fear, for you are my sons. If strangers eat at my table, much more shall you who are my lawful sons."
>
> And then the king sent a message to his beautiful wife in the desert to have all her sons come in to be a part of his court.

Francis immediately went to Innocent III and related this parable. Then he explained to the Pope, "Very holy father, I am this poor woman whom God in His love has deigned to make beautiful and of whom He has been pleased to have lawful sons. The King of Kings has told me that He will provide for all the sons which He may have of me, for if He sustains bastards, how much more His legitimate sons."

129

This parable and Francis' interpretation finally convinced Innocent to approve the rule that would establish the Franciscan order. Or to put it another way, God's direction of Francis' thoughts in answer to prayer not only changed the mind of a Pope, but the course of Christian history as well.

Now before you draw the conclusion that this method only works in "religious" business—let me give you a more recent example from the world of *secular* business. A friend of mine, Harold McNaughton, was driving down a freeway outside Los Angeles one day, and really enjoying a prayer time conversation with the Lord. Up till this one particular moment, it had been a "one way" conversation, with Harold just praising the Lord and thanking Him for a lot of things, occasionally voicing some concern or other.

Suddenly Harold felt he got a distinct instruction from the Lord, so strong that it seemed audible. "I want you to buy land in this very area that you're passing."

Startled as he was, Harold looked around him. This was wasteland! It was undeveloped, dry, apparently good for nothing. Why in the world would God want him to buy land *here?* Still, the impression had been so strong that Harold began to do some checking, and found that he could buy or option hundreds of acres in that area for very little. So he did.

Within a matter of months, it was announced that the new Los Angeles International Airport would be built in that very area! The value of Harold's property skyrocketed.

Does the process of listening suddenly sound more practical?

Not all thought-directed answers to prayer are this dramatic, of course. More often, I feel that the Lord weights one alternative more heavily than another, so that it just seems more reasonable to us. Sometimes a totally new and surprising course of action may suggest itself to you, and with such a clarity that you'll realize this may very well be God's answer. If so, try it! Commit it to the Lord, tell Him that you believe this is His answer, and ask Him to help you implement it. If you're not absolutely sure, ask Him to make it obvious to you right away if you have jumped to the wrong conclusion. He'll work with you, and teach you how to more accurately and confidently hear His voice.

I've found that He'll even use my imagination! I've already said that the wandering mind can become a serious enemy of effective prayer—but then, creativity is a gift from God, and an active imagination *can* be harnessed and used by the Lord to get a point across very quickly.

I recall a recent incident involving one of my musicians. I was having some problems with his work, and I knew I was going to have to have a talk with him, but I decided to spend some time praying about the problem. I presented the issue to God and just lingered on it for a few moments, and soon I found I was picturing talking to the fellow and running through a complete dialogue I might have with him. Then I thought, "This is great! This is exactly the way I should approach him." And sure enough, the mental image the Lord had given me in prayer was almost like a script; what could have been a very unpleasant encounter was handled very smoothly and happily—almost like a rerun on television!

I'm just on the first frontiers in exploring how God can use my imagination, and I know there's always the danger that a spiritually creative mind can turn from helpful and exciting soaring with God to useless flights of fancy or even dead ends. But I know God has spoken to me through free mental imagery, and I wonder if maybe that wasn't part of what Jesus experienced when He took time for those long periods of meditation which sometimes lasted all night. Perhaps He allowed the Father to show Him how to deal with people, situations and issues through just such movements of the imagination.

After all, God had to *imagine* the world before He created it—and we have inherited some of that ability from Him!

—*Physical events.* God answers us not only through our minds but also by causing things to happen in the world around us. He may effect the healing of a sick body; He may bring rain on parched ground; or He may cause a storm to be stilled.

Not long ago I was praying earnestly about a new idea I had for a record company I own. To develop this new opportunity, it was necessary for me to talk to a very important man with a large corporation. This man is always on the go, and though I left phone messages for him, and him for me, we could never seem to make contact. I kept praying. Within a matter of a couple of days I got on a plane to head across the country—*and sat down next to the very man I wanted to talk to!* Neither of us knew the other was within a thousand miles, but the fact that we had been brought together this way gave us both a special sense of the "rightness" of our meeting.

A friend of mine who lives in New York is the husband of a very capable teacher. When she's got some rough going in her classroom, he prays for her. "The other day, I prayed that the Lord would do one of two things for a kid in my wife's class," he said. "She had a very difficult class this semester, by the way—some of the kids were really off the wall. So I prayed the Lord would either take this one rebellious girl out of that class or change her heart. Within two days the girl was gone from the class. At about the same time, I prayed for a disruptive little boy my wife was teaching—that He would either remove him or make him responsive and helpful. Almost immediately his attitude started to change. I knew God would act one way or another in this situation because I was convinced personally that something had to be done for the benefit of those unruly kids, and for the entire class, and for my wife as well."

God can move mountains—or other people—in answer to our prayers.

—*Words of other people.* Sometimes, after I have asked the Lord to give me a specific answer, I go about my business and suddenly someone—perhaps Shirley or one of my daughters or a friend—will say something to me completely out of the blue that will be the answer I was seeking! The person who spoke the words may not have any idea that he or she has spoken to me for God, but I recognize it, and I just silently thank Him. Don't get the idea that this is "kooky"; throughout the Bible, God spoke through all sorts of Prophets and ordinary people as well, and He'll communicate the same way with us today—if we'll just put ourselves in a position to hear Him. Sometimes the most "religious" people are the hardest of hearing; in the Book of Numbers there is the account of God speaking to His Prophet—through a mule!

I always hate to miss a service at my home congregation, The Church on the Way, in Van Nuys, California. Almost invariably either the minister, Jack Hayford, or someone in my little prayer group will say something that is aimed directly at me and a decision that I need to make. It's absolutely uncanny. And it's not just me; almost everybody I've ever brought to one of the services has asked, "Did you tell someone I was coming? Everything that minister said was for *me!*"

I always say, "The only one I told you were coming was God. Did you hear Him talking to you today?"

The Lord spoke to me once on the radio! I wrote about it in *A Miracle a Day Keeps the Devil Away,* but I think it will bear repeating here. I'd come in from a late-night engagement and crawled into bed bone-weary. Shirley stirred in the darkness long enough to ask me what time she should wake me up, and I answered, "I've got a very important nine o'clock meeting. Better wake me up at eight-fifteen." Shirley murmured, "You'll never make a nine o'clock meeting if you wake up at eight-fifteen, and you know it." I answered, "I've just got to get some sleep, honey. Not a minute before eight-fifteen, okay?"

Lying there in the darkness, just seconds away from sleep, I had to agree that Shirley was right. There was little likelihood that I would wake up at eight-fifteen, jump out of bed and get ready soon enough to make a very important nine o'clock meeting. What was I to do? In the softest of whispers, I prayed: "Jesus, are You still awake? Would You help me get up at eight-fifteen and get ready and to a meeting on time? I know I can't do it without Your help—so I'll thank You in advance. Good night, Lord." And I was out like a light.

Shirley was up by seven, got the children off to school and was about to wake me up at eight-fifteen, when she did something she had never done before. She was listening to Kathryn Kuhlman on the radio, and this lady preacher was reading from the fifth chapter of Ephesians. Shirley didn't want to miss what she was about to say, so the thought occurred to wake me up by turning on the stereo in our house. There was a speaker right by our bed where I was sawing logs, and she could accomplish two things at once: she could keep listening to Kathryn Kuhlman and wake me up at the same time! So she punched on the stereo (which was already at this particular station) and as the radio warmed up, Shirley cranked it up very loud so it would blare in my ear, and it did, just as Miss Kuhlman was arriving at the four-teenth verse of the fifth chapter of Ephesians. Lying there in my deep stupor, the first thing I heard was

Kathryn Kuhlman's voice, very loudly saying, "AWAKE, THOU THAT SLEEPEST!"

I woke up with my hair standing on end—realized what had happened, jumped through my morning routine in record time, and made my nine o'clock meeting! I laughed about it later—but I realized that there were just too many variables in that situation for it to have been a coincidence. I don't know *how* He arranged that wake-up service—but I know that He did it.

I could give you hundreds of other examples. But if you're asking God for an answer, don't be surprised if it comes through the lips of someone else. It's another way He has of making us sensitive to each other, and weaving us together.

—*Open and closed doors.* Are you willing to take no for an answer? Sometimes that's the best one available.

Occasionally I've been asked to pray with someone who found his job intolerable; he wanted out, and felt that God must have something better for him somewhere else. I've usually asked the same questions: "Have you prayed about it; do you know of another specific opportunity? Has the Lord indicated *where* else you might go? Have you considered that maybe the Lord has you exactly where He wants you right now?" That last one is usually not very popular.

It's quite possible that God wants to change something, but it's not your job. It may be *you*; or it may be someone working with you, and God wants to use you as His instrument. A very good way to test God's direction is to ask Him to provide an open door elsewhere if He wants you to move. If it doesn't open—stay put!

A related idea involves what some people call "putting out a fleece"—after the lamb's fleece that the Old Testament Hebrew leader Gideon put on the ground to ascertain definitely what God's will was for him. An angel of God had appeared to Gideon, a lowly winepress worker, and told him he had been chosen to *lead Israel in battle against her enemies.* Talk about a new job! Gideon was incredulous, and he asked for a sign, which the angel provided. But Gideon wasn't the most courageous of men, and when the time came for him to actually embark on a military campaign, he hesitated.

"You say that you have decided to use me to rescue Israel," Gideon said to God in Judges 6:36–40. "Well, I am putting some wool (RSV says a 'fleece of wool') on the ground where we thresh the wheat. If in the morning there is dew only on the wool but not on the ground, then I will know that you are going to use me to rescue Israel." (Today's English Version)

Sure enough, there was enough dew on the wool for Gideon to wring it out and fill a bowl with water the next morning, and the ground around the fleece was dry. But Gideon still wasn't satisfied.

"Don't be angry with me; let me speak just once more," he said to God. "Please let me make one more test with the wool. This time let the wool be dry, and the ground be wet."

And once again God responded exactly in accordance with Gideon's request. Now some people say that this incident just reflects Gideon's lack of faith in God's loving patience with him in demonstrating again and again that Gideon had indeed been divinely chosen to lead Israel against the Midianites and other enemy tribes. And certainly, Gideon does exhibit an exceptionally cautious nature for one who had been visited by an angel and had witnessed some other unusual signs from God. But the writer of the book of Hebrews cites him as one of the great Old Testament models of faith (Hebrews 11:32) so he must have been on to something!

Let's face it; there are times when you just don't *know* what God's will is. And if you're honest with yourself, and you really want what's best, I believe God will show you. He did for Gideon and He will for you and me. My friend Harald Bredesen advises, "Make it easy on yourself, and hard on God." What does he mean? Well, if you're in that uneasy job situation, for example, you might ask the Lord to open up a new situation for you, one that's unmistakably right for you—and by a certain deadline. God can do that, you know. It might be hard for anyone else to arrange things that way, but not for Him. If the new job opens up, go rejoicing. If it doesn't, stay the same way. If the answer is "no," you can be confident that you're where God wants you, and that He will work with you to achieve your goals (and His) where you are—and I can promise you that the rewards will be greater than if you arbitrarily pulled up stakes and left.

"Putting our fleeces" certainly isn't the only way to discern God's will—but it can be one of them.

—*The Bible.* Now we're down to basics, the most infallible and dependable way of hearing from God. There is no more sure method of knowing God's will in any situation or getting more precise guidance, than to read what He has inspired and spoken and published in that beautiful black book, so accessible to every one of us. Though God understands our ignorance, and realizes that we can't assimilate all the truth in the Bible right away; and though He will, on occasion, speak to us through some other means; He will not forever subsidize our willful neglect of His own written word.

More strongly than anything else in this book, *I urge you to make daily Bible reading a pattern for the rest of your life.*

Like countless others, including myself, you'll be amazed at the way God speaks to you through your own daily Bible reading—often right on a specific target! Remember, I'm not talking about that random emergency method of just opening the Bible with your eyes shut, and poking your finger into the first passage that opens up. There's the story about a man who did that, and his eyes fell quickly on the passage "And Judas went and hanged himself." The man quickly tried his method again, and this time his finger settled on the passage, "Go and do likewise!"

No, I'm talking about diligent study, a constant and open-minded exposure to the revealed truth in God's Word. There's no substitute, and there's no shortcut. Listen to what God tells you through James:

"If you want to know what God wants you to do, ask Him, and He will gladly tell you, for He is always ready to give a bountiful supply of *wisdom* to all who ask Him; He will not resent it. But when you ask Him, be sure that you really expect Him to tell you, for a doubtful mind will be as unsettled as a wave of the sea that is driven and tossed by the wind; and every decision you then make will be uncertain, as you turn first this way, and then that. If you don't ask with faith, don't expect the Lord to give you any solid answer." (James 1:5–8)

Wisdom—that's what we're after. Please read the whole eighth chapter of Proverbs. Its author is Solomon, the wisest and most successful king Israel ever had. That whole chapter is about wisdom, and here are a couple of excerpts: "Wisdom and good judgment live together, for wisdom knows where to discover knowledge and under-standing." And here is another gem: "I, Wisdom, give good advice and common sense. Because of my strength, kings reign in power. I show the judges who is right and who is wrong. Rulers rule well with my help. I love all who love me. Those who search for me shall surely find me. Unending riches, honour, justice and righteousness are mine to distribute. My gifts are better than the purest gold or sterling silver! My paths are those of justice and right. Those who love and follow me are indeed wealthy. I fill their treasuries."

The wisdom and knowledge of all the ages, the very best that God has to offer, is distilled in that precious Book. Paul writes, "The whole Bible was given to us by inspiration from God and is useful to teach us what is true and to make us realize what is wrong in our lives; it straightens us out and helps us to do what is right. *It is God's way of making us well-prepared at every point, fully equipped to do good to everyone.*" (Second Timothy 3)

Don't you want to be truly wise? I sure do. I don't always want to live on the brink of emergency, always looking for a panic button to push. I don't always want to be crying "Help!" when I could have avoided the trouble in the first place. No, I want to be a mature man, I want to know my Father and His will well enough that I can make wise judgments in all of life's situations. And if I *am* confronted with something new and unexpected, and I really don't know what God's specific answer might be, I want to be able to sit down with His Word and find the answer in black and white.

That, I think, is the ultimate in maturity.

Lawyers do it that way. Doctors do it that way. Even mechanics and plumbers do it that way. When these professional people face a knotty problem, they take out the instruction manuals, the books that they *know* contain the answers, and dig them out! After enough knotty problems, and enough sessions with the books, they reach the place where they have most of the answers already in their heads—but that doesn't happen without hard work and study.

But what businessman worth his salt is afraid of hard work and study? That's always been the secret of success! It's always been the prime ingredient of winning!

I'm thinking again about the conversation I had with Bob Ringer, author of *Looking Out for No. 1.* "I sometimes get the idea that religious people see themselves as just a bunch of windup dolls running around and doing God's will," he said. "But do you think He really expects us to be like that? The whole idea seems so trivial."

"No," I replied, "God doesn't want a bunch of automatons—*he wants sons and daughters who will grow up to be like Him.* But even with little children, you have to give them some rules to live by so they can learn to obey and trust you and also so that it will be easier to protect them. Kids often wish their parents would let them do anything they want, but the parents know kids can't grow up properly that way. Children need discipline and instruction. Then, as the child develops mature judgment, he doesn't need to be told what to do. In the same way, God wants people to grow up through His discipline to be responsible adults, and not just spoiled brats."

I can remember several times when my own father answered me with just a look, or a raised eyebrow—even silence. When my request was trivial or out of line, that's all it took. God employs that same method sometimes.

Professor Howard Hendricks of the Dallas Theological Seminary tells about the time when he was a young, single pastor in the Midwest; he would stand outside the church door every Sunday morning and greet those who had attended the service as they filed by. And every Sunday morning, the same elderly mother and her daughter would arrange to be the last ones out, and the mother would always say, "I'm praying for you, pastor— that you'll see God's will and marry my daughter."

After telling this anecdote in his classes, Hendricks would look his students straight in the eye and ask, "Have you ever thanked God for *unanswered* prayer?"

I chuckle every time I think about this incident, but there's a serious point that Professor Hendricks was making: God may refuse to give us what we want because what we want may be the worst thing in the world, for us—or for someone else. Also, God sometimes says "no" because He wants to teach us spiritual endurance and He knows that a little trouble may be just the right prescription to hasten our spiritual maturity.

I know that's true, because God says it! "We can rejoice, too, when we run into problems and trials for we know that they are good for us—they help us learn to be patient. And patience develops strength of character in us and helps us trust God more each time we use it until finally our hope and faith are strong and steady." (Romans 5)

I'll tell you, I want to fly with a pilot that's already been through some rough weather, maybe even a couple of forced landings; if I'm going into open-heart surgery, I want a doctor who's already had some close calls and maybe lost a patient or two, because he knows what to look out for; and I think I'd rather have as a business partner a man who's had some hard knocks and failures under his belt. I love what Bill Walton said when UCLA lost its first basketball game in over fifty outings. The big redheaded center, known for few words, answered when they asked him how he felt, "I think I learned more tonight than from all the games we won. I've heard that you learn more from failure than success, anyway." Big Bill was bigger than his announced six-ten height that night.

So, if you're really serious about winning through prayer, accomplishing the worthwhile goals in your life with God's help, pray. Pray regularly and diligently. Then listen; listen with your heart and your head and your spirit. Check God's Word, and dig for the answers there. One way or the other, rest assured—God will answer!

11 God's Special Communication Codes

Would you like to take a breather? Would you like to pause and get refreshed a moment before we press on?

As I look over the ground we've covered already, I realize we've come a long way. I've assumed that we were starting from zero, considering prayer as if it were a totally new concept to you. If that be true, we've come a long way, and you might just be starting to tire somewhat, perhaps wondering if this is worth all the effort and brain-strain.

"Why all the hokus-pokus?" you may be asking. "Why all the difficulty in communicating with God? If He really wants to talk with me, if He really wants me to hear from Him and understand Him, why doesn't he just talk out loud or better yet, write His instructions in the sky for all of us, so that there can't be any mistake? Why should there be this difficulty, this hit-and-miss method, this *work*, just to talk with God?"

That's a very good, intelligent question. You may have

been asking it long before now—and that's why I thought we ought to take a "spiritual breather."

I hope you'll pause with me, and literally do what I am about to suggest. Sit comfortably in your chair, try to wash everything else out of your mind for a moment, and take a few deep breaths. We've talked about this briefly already, and I'll explain it further in a moment, but first just relax. Ask the Lord, in the name of His Son Jesus, to share His breath with you, to fill you with His Holy Spirit as you take several more deep breaths. Exhale slowly, thanking Him in your own words for revealing Himself to you and quickening the desire in you to pray and to understand Him better. Forget your specific goals for a moment; just invite and enjoy His presence. It's very important that you do this before we take our discussion any further. If you don't, there is a strong likelihood you really won't understand the rest of this chapter.

There's a reason for the mystery about prayer. There's a reason for the difficulty, there's a reason for limited understanding, there's a reason even for supernatural "coded messages."

There is a war going on. And we're in the middle of it!

The whole Bible, from Genesis through Revelation, is this detailed story of an all-out elemental war between God and Satan. Oh, I know; in spite of all the movies like *The Exorcist, The Omen, The Amityville Horror,* and the countless books and TV movies about demons and Satanic invasions, it's still not popular among "practical"-thinking people to admit the existence of a real devil. It's hard enough to admit there is a real God— but even that's more fashionable, within limits, than to admit the reality of a real Beelzebub with horns on his head and a long, pointed tail and a pitchfork, running around trying to tempt us and steal our souls away. "The devil made me do it" was one of comedian Flip Wilson's favorite lines—and it never failed to get a big laugh.

But the same Bible that talks about God, about a messiah named Jesus, that offers all the promises about winning through prayer, talks openly from beginning to the end about an adversary, a fallen angelic being named Lucifer, whose announced objective is to destroy God's highest creation—mankind—and in so doing, attempt to elevate himself to God's status. Whether it appeals to your intellect or not, you can't accept God or the Bible without also accepting the existence of Lucifer.

God has given him another name, Satan, which means "adversary." In just the same way, he gave Jesus another name, Christ or Messiah, which means "the anointed one." You get the picture, don't you? We're talking about the heavyweight fight of all time!

"But what's this got to do with me? I thought we were talking about prayer, about achieving my goals, about winning. Let's get back on the subject, Boone!"

Believe me, I'm still very much on the subject.

I just talked recently to a handsome ex-naval officer who commanded a destroyer during the Second World War. He was in the thick of the battle in the Pacific, as the air and sea battles raged around the last major islands, Saipan and Guadalcanal, leading up to the invasion and surrender of Japan. After talking at some length on the horrors and the complexities of that part of the war, he made this statement, "But it all got a lot easier *after we broke their codes.* From then on we knew what they were planning to do, and could beat them to it."

We had our codes, of course, and so did the Germans and the Russians. Why? Because in any war there is an advantage to being able to communicate without the enemy understanding what you're saying, even if he hears you. Secrecy and surprise have always played a big part in war, bringing with them spying, intrigue and all sorts of cloak and dagger stuff.

For this very reason, Jesus spoke in coded messages—called parables. When I first saw this, it stunned me. But it's true! Check it out in Matthew 13. Right after Jesus had told His well-known parable called "The Sower," His disciples asked Him (the Living Bible version), "Why do you always use these hard-to-understand illustrations?"

Then He explained to them that only they were permitted to understand about the Kingdom of Heaven, and others were not.

"For him who has will more be given," He told them, "and he will have great plenty; but from him who has not (understanding), even the little he has will be taken away. That is why I use these illustrations, *so people will hear and see but not understand.*" (Matthew 13:10–13)

Does that mystify you, as it did me? Don't you wonder why Jesus would purposely speak in riddles, in veiled messages, intentionally hiding much of His truth from people who were listening? I certainly did, and immediately made a study of it. And I want to share some of the results of that study with you right now. You need to read that whole chapter in Matthew, to begin to get a fuller picture of the situation. In His parable about the Sower, scattering seed (God's truth) on various kinds of soil, Jesus says, "The hard path where some of the seeds fell represents the heart of a person who hears the Good News about the Kingdom and doesn't understand it; *then Satan comes and snatches away the seeds from his heart.*" Whether we like it or not, Jesus is very plainly talking about an active agency, an enemy infiltrator who is able to steal secrets right out of our hearts and minds! And because he's invisible and largely dismissed as mythical, he can be very effective. He can throw up barricades, he can jam our prayer frequencies, he can

145

transmit counterfeit messages, put up "detour" signs to head us off in the wrong directions, and even plant landmines of distraction and deception in our way!

Again from the parable "The ground covered with thistles represents a man who hears the message, but *the cares of this life and his longing for money* choke out God's Word, and he does less for God." See how it works? If you begin to see things from the Bible perspective, you can understand much more clearly why prayer can be difficult, why most of us just never "have time" for reading the Bible or relationship with God, why everything around us seems to portray God's plan as irrational, impractical and unworkable. The simple truth is this: Any man who decides he wants to develop a genuine relationship with God and to communicate with Him personally will meet with premeditated, highly effective, diabolic opposition! You can count on it!

Chances are you'll find many more demands on your time; your business will become more complex, perhaps even suddenly more successful; family problems and pressures may accelerate; all kinds of burdens and distractions will come at you from unexpected directions. You may even get the feeling you have become a *target* of some kind—and you have! When a man gets serious about praying, about partnership with God, he automatically becomes dangerous to God's enemy, Satan. But old Lucifer is too cunning, too experienced, to make a frontal attack, exposing who he is and his intentions for your soul. Instead, he'll just try to muddy the water, discredit the whole idea of faith and prayer, distract and confuse you, and try to get you to give the whole idea up.

Knowing this, Jesus laid a very careful strategy, and followed a Master Plan which included revealing truth only on certain wavelengths, and even then coding many of His messages, so that only those who knew the code could understand. He taught things like "Don't let your right hand know what your left hand is doing"; "Go into your closet and pray in secret, so that your Heavenly Father can reward you openly"; "Don't cast your pearls before swine, lest they turn and rend you." He was teaching these things *for our protection*, because He knew that we'd not be allowed to blithely obey God and pursue a life of practical faith without fierce and treacherous opposition.

The Bible actually says, in First Corinthians 2, "We speak of God's secret wisdom, a wisdom that has been hidden and that God destined for our glory before time began. *None of the rulers of this age understood it, for if they had*, they would have not crucified the Lord of Glory." The astounding fact is that God completely fooled Satan and his demonic horde, who thought they were *defeating* Jesus when they crucified Him, only to find that they had played perfectly into God's own prearranged plan for man's salvation! And even though Jesus plainly told His disciples what He had come for, and how it was going to be accomplished, He used language that neither they nor Satan really understood— until it had been accomplished. I really get excited, thinking about that! Paul, the writer of Corinthians, continues: "But God has revealed it to us by his Spirit.

"The Spirit searches all things, even the deep things of God. For who among men knows the thoughts of a man except the man's spirit within him? In the same way no one knows the thoughts of God except the Spirit of God. *We have not received the spirit of the world but the Spirit who is from God*, that we may understand what God has really given us. This is what we speak, *not in words taught us by human wisdom but in words taught by the Spirit, expressing spiritual truths in spiritual words.*"

Spiritual words. What does he mean by that?

Listen to him a little further. "The man without the spirit does not accept the things that come from the Spirit of God, for they are foolishness to him, and he cannot understand them, *because they are spiritually discerned.*" (Second Corinthians 2:7–15)

Do you see why I wanted you to take a few deep spiritual breaths at the beginning of this chapter? I have really prayed that you and I would be filled with God's own Spirit, that our minds would be animated and activated by His own intelligence, so that we could understand the truth of these scriptures. He clearly declares that no MIT or Harvard PhD is going to understand these truths on a truly intellectual level; in fact, man's mind actually is at war with God's Spirit.

And so we come to the crux, the central point of this whole chapter. In addition to the other kinds of prayer that we've talked about, the various frequencies that involve speaking to the Lord and listening for His response, there are two other channels that are more sophisticated, supernaturally, and therefore less known and employed.

I'm talking about speaking in tongues—and meditation.

There's no way I can adequately discuss these two profound prayer channels in this chapter, but I can't leave them out either. Not while we're talking about powerful prayer, the kind of prayer that really gets results. So we'll talk about them just briefly, and at least establish some of the reasons that I believe they're so vital. I discuss my own early experience with tongues or special God-given prayer language in intimate detail in my book *A New Song.*

You may ask, "Oh, yes, I've heard about speaking in tongues. What is that?"

I'm sure no description is adequate. Some things you really can't understand until you *experience* them.

But the Bible talks about "divers," or diverse, tongues; there are several categories. One is a phenomenon that occurred on the day of Pentecost in Jerusalem, when Jesus' Kingdom was established; His disciples actually spoke a variety of languages they'd never learned, but which the people around them from other countries understood! Another is "tongues and interpretation," a method by which God speaks to a worshiping group, first empowering a believer to speak in an unknown language, and then giving another believer the ability to interpret the message in the language that all the rest of the worshipers understand; and the messages are invariably instructional, beneficial and uplifting for the whole group. A third is a purely devotional language, by which a person "speaks mysteries to God." This last one is the most common, and I have found it to be a magnificent channel for praise, devotion and an infinite variety of feelings that I want to express to my Heavenly Father— but don't have English words for.

As mysterious and misunderstood as these prayer languages are, I hope you've caught a glimpse of their immense practicality. Just as Jesus was on this Earth, God is still in the business of communicating and revealing mysteries to His believing children—while at the same time hiding them from His enemies in the spirit realm. These languages are not something you learn, either by technique or through study. They are *given* by the Holy Spirit, and must be experienced as an act of faith. Lots of people feel you have to be in some kind of ecstatic state to speak in tongues, but my experience and study tells me this isn't so. There *have* been cases in which people spoke ecstatically, but Paul indicates in First Corinthians 14 that "the spirit is subject to the Prophet," and that speaking in tongues is speaking "not to men but to God," and "no man understands him."

My dad is a building contractor, and a very practical man. He wasn't at all sure that speaking in tongues was for today; he'd always believed it was a first century phenomenon. But after he had studied the New Testament carefully to "straighten Pat out," he came to the conclusion that there seemed to be no time barrier imposed on the workings of the Holy Spirit. He told the Lord in his own private prayer time that he was willing to experience this spiritual language, if the Lord wanted him to, but that he wasn't going to try to "work it up." One morning, in the middle of his own early devotional period, he was thanking the Lord for all the ways He'd blessed our family, when a great joy and gratitude welled up inside of him. The feeling was so intense that he felt his throat constricting, almost painfully. Daddy says he'd felt that kind of thing before, but that men aren't supposed to cry, so he would always literally "choke it back." This morning he didn't—and in a moment of simple release, found his voice giving utterance to a babble of words that he didn't understand; he only knew that he was giving a perfect vocal expression to what he felt inside. It was a beautiful experience! Ever since, he's learned that he can "speak mysteries" to the Lord any time he wants to, and that his own spiritual life has grown immeasurably.

We're in deep water here; I know that. This is not an easy subject to explore, and I may have moved way beyond your interests already. But any serious student of prayer and the Bible teaching on prayer must eventually come to a consideration of this mysterious prayer language. The New Testament writer Paul, an extremely intelligent and learned man, writes more about it than anyone else in the Bible. I hope you'll read the whole fourteenth chapter of First Corinthians, in a modern translation like the New International Version. Though this brilliant man said, "I speak in tongues more than any of you," his plea is for balance and order. He knew that the human tendency (then and now) is to get so excited about this new ability to communicate with God that ordinary rational prayer might be almost abandoned. And that happens in a lot of religious circles today; folks get so excited about "tongues" that they neglect all the other precious channels of prayer and spiritual growth.

Don't let this happen to you! If you do move on into this new dimension, if you ask the Lord to fill you completely with His Holy Spirit and find that that Spirit overflows into this wonderful coded language, take care to follow Paul's formula: "So what shall I do? I will pray with my spirit, but I will also pray with my mind; I will sing with my spirit, but I will also sing with my mind."

That's been my formula. My first experience in tongues was "singing in the spirit"; thus my *New Song*. I soon discovered that I could sing in this prayer language, and more enthusiastically in English as well. I also learned that I could pray in this supernatural language, and more intelligently in English as well.

Oral Roberts built his university this way!

Oral Roberts University, as you may know, is one of the outstanding and most modern centers of learning in the world. And it was built by a man who never graduated from a university himself! Oral told me that the Lord had showed him, over thirty years ago, that someday he would build a college; He didn't tell Oral how, and Oral just tabled the thought until he got further instruction. Twenty-five years went by—and in a private prayer time, Oral says he heard the Lord's voice:

151

"I want you to build a college, a university, and I want you to build it the same way that I created the Earth—out of nothing."

And that was all. There was no further instruction.

What would you do? Oral knew he had a commission, but he didn't have a blueprint. He prayed earnestly, asking the Lord for more details, but he heard nothing in response. Soon after, he was with a mutual friend, Ralph Wilkerson of Melodyland Christian Center in Los Angeles, and he told him about his dilemma.

Ralph listened, talked it over with Oral, and advised, "Let's pray about it, Oral. Let's pray in the Spirit (in tongues), because I know you've already prayed a whole lot with your understanding." Oral agreed.

Ralph began to pray fervently with his prayer language—but Oral just remained silent with his head bowed.

"Don't you want to pray in the Spirit?" Ralph asked.

"I'm waiting, but it's not happening," Oral replied.

"What do you mean it's not happening? Just do it!"

"Ralph, I've spoken in tongues a number of times, but it's been in periods of stress or exaltation," Oral replied. "I'm willing, but I'm just waiting for it to happen."

"Well, let's talk about that a little bit," Ralph said. "Paul says in First Corinthians 14, 'I *will* pray with the spirit and I *will* pray with the mind also.' It's an act of your will. Certainly, you might speak in tongues in moments of extreme joy or pain or grief or need, and those times it may seem involuntary. But your body is subject to your spirit, so you can speak to God in tongues whenever you desire to do it, no matter how you happen to be feeling."

So Oral, his emotions virtually "in neutral," began to speak rather haltingly in tongues. For quite some time, he and Ralph prayed together in this supernatural coded language, the Holy Spirit working with them as He promised in Romans 8, "In the same way, the Spirit helps us in our weakness. We do not know what we ought to pray, but the Spirit Himself intercedes for us *with groanings that words cannot express.* And he who searches our hearts knows the mind of the Spirit because the Spirit intercedes for the saints in accordance with God's will."

See how practical this really is? The Lord Himself, knowing how limited our intelligence is, takes the desire of our hearts and our willing voices *and actually words our prayers for us, in a language that Lucifer can't understand!*

Not that the intellect is negated; far from it. Praying in the Spirit can make the mind much more fruitful. Oral is a living demonstration of that; after he and Ralph had spent considerable time praying in tongues, a very clear impression emerged in Oral's mind that he should begin the university by establishing the Oral Roberts Foundation—and that he should donate everything he had to that Foundation. He immediately obeyed, giving his house, furniture, his small bank account and all his other material possessions away to the Oral Roberts University Foundation. And from this humble beginning, others were led by God to contribute large and small amounts into the same Foundation, and a university was born.

Oral tells me that from that moment on, he decided to spend a considerable amount of his own private devotional time following the same pattern: praying first in the Spirit, in his supernatural language, and then with his understanding, in English. He believes that's the right order, and so do I—evidently so did Paul. Quite frequently, Oral finds that his English prayers are far more exciting and incisive and "on target" *because* he has stirred up his inner man spiritually, and already agreed with God and His specific will through their supernatural communication. As a result, there exists in Tulsa, Oklahoma, a university that would confound Andrew Carnegie and Cornelius Vanderbilt!

And the *best part* is that Oral Roberts University is teaching thousands of our finest young men and women how to pray and to win in the same way! In addition to the finest in the liberal arts, in education and the fields of business and medicine, every ORU student is taught a deep reverence for God and is schooled in the techniques of discerning God's will and praying powerfully. These young men and women are going to alter the course of history and change our world! They're being taught to combine the finest in intellectual achievement with the highest and the deepest in spiritual maturity. What a combination!

I have to conclude our discussion about speaking in tongues. Just a few words of summation and we'll move on. The Bible teaches that there are countless languages and vocal possibilities in the world, and none without the potential of meaning. In my own sphere of experience, I've talked to lots of people whose prayer language came in some unique way—in laughter, in tears, in clicking sounds, in singing or moaning or what might sound like meaningless babble. But regardless of the initial sounds or words, their languages have diversified and developed in direct proportion to their spiritual commitments, their maturity and their desire to have meaningful communication with the Lord. I tell you this because your own initial prayer language experience might seem disappointing and inconsequential to you, and I want you to keep in mind your motive, not the results—and God, who sees your heart, will be your language teacher. Trust Him.

And why does God provide this special coded language for us? To make up for the shortcomings of human language and our ability to put into words what we feel and really need; to encourage a childlike dependence and trust in the Lord to make up for our inadequacies, instead of a dependence on our own meager intellects; and to give us a "hotline" directly to the heart of God that can't be jammed or scrambled, or even understood by our Satanic adversary.

But here's a final warning: don't dabble in tongues. This ability is only given by the Holy Spirit, and *only* for the purpose of equipping true sons and daughters of the Living God with power to serve—and to win.

Meditation may seem tame after the discussion of tongues—but it's not. I'm talking about *Christian* meditation, which focuses on some passage or promise from God, revealed in His Scripture. *I'm not talking about transcendental meditation!* TM, as taught by the Maharishi, is a Hindu religion, and revolves around the acceptance of Hindu gods and Hindu philosophy. The Bible soundly condemns this, particularly in the First Commandment, which thunders, *"Thou shalt have no other gods before Me"!*

No, I'm not talking about TM; and I'm not talking about a kind of aimless trance or daydreaming, in which the mind is just allowed to "wander." I'm talking about the person, described in the First Psalm, "whose delight is in the law of the Lord, and *on His law he meditates day and night."* David, a man after God's own heart, reveals a deep secret of their relationship in Psalm 119:148: "My eyes are awake before the watches of the night, *that I may meditate upon thy promise."*

See the difference? It's not just aimless "blank-mindedness," some languid escape from mental pressure. No, profitable meditation takes a shining gold nugget and turns it slowly, inspecting it from many angles and admiring its many facets. You see, God's Word is "radioactive"; you can't get close to it in any prolonged way without being exposed to its radiation, its effects. When you sit and meditate on one of God's gems, whether you're driving along or alone in a room, you'll often experience a sudden illumination, a piercing shaft of revelation that will excite and instruct you. It's truly an amazing phenomenon, unique in human experience. You cannot exhaust the meaning of any single Bible passage—I challenge you to try it!

Why, Jesus actually said, "Heaven and Earth will pass away—but My Words will never pass away!" There's such an enduring and unfathomable nature in God's revealed truth that gold and diamonds and even plutonium crumble to dust beside one of God's Scriptural gems.

The Prophet Isaiah promised, "But they that wait upon the Lord shall renew their strength. They shall mount up with wings like eagles; they shall run and not be weary; they shall walk and not faint." (Isaiah 40:31) And one of the ways to truly "wait upon the Lord" is to meditate on the Word. And just look at the practical benefits!

Friend, I hope you know by now that I'm not interested in a monklike life. We've been concentrating on *doing*—on action and achievement and accomplishing real goals in a contemporary world. But frantic activity, apart from quiet planning and meditation, will eventually lead to ulcers, mistakes and frustration. Isn't it much more reasonable, in the short and long run of things, to quietly research and lay out a workable plan—one that you've devised with the Lord's guidance—and then methodically accomplish the goal with God's own supernatural assistance?

A final note: Moishe Rosen, leader of the Jews for Jesus, spends an hour or more in prayer each morning and devotes part of this time to "holding" one short verse or passage of Scripture in his mind. He meditates on the verse from different perspectives and allows God to show him personal ways of applying that verse in his own life and in the lives of others. Frequently, as a result of this meditation, he may find himself thinking and praying about one of his many acquaintances around the country. He might also feel moved to put his thoughts into immediate action by writing a short note to one of these friends—and to facilitate this practice he keeps plenty of blank postcards on hand.

These "prayer postcards" are a perfect springboard from meditation into action. I myself often write notes so that I won't lose or forget what I've learned in meditation. Good idea.

Now we're ready to move on.

You've got some powerful arrows in your quiver. Let's get out on the range and point them at some specific targets!

PART III
Exploring the Frontiers of Prayer Power

12 The Language of Love Is Learned at Home

Human relationships are fragile things.

Marriage, statistically, appears to be a doomed institution. An analysis of the most recent census indicates that *at least half of America's children* will be raised in one-parent families! Divorce and "modern life-styles" are taking their tragic toll.

As the pace quickens and the complexity of life seems to multiply geometrically, few relationships of any kind seem to flourish. The "old days" are gone—and with them most of the traditional morals and ethics and traditions that held our society together.

Prayer was legislated out of our schools—only to be replaced by pot and rampant sex, v.d. and occult religions. Millions of America's finest families "outgrew" Sunday school and church—and have long since disintegrated.

Frankly, I don't see how *any* friendship or marriage can survive today without making God a "third party," through prayer.

Look at the ordinary husband and wife today. In the midst of all the busyness of earning a living and raising a family, they find they can handle the mundane affairs, all the thousands of details, but often find it difficult to communicate about the things that really matter to them personally, way down deep inside. When the real issues do surface, they often lead to conflict and argument, pain and alienation. That's the normal situation; but a healthy prayer life, in which both partners feel free to talk to God in each other's presence, can make a dynamic difference. Praying together, the husband and wife can deal honestly with the most crucial issues and agree with God's will for the growth of their own relationship, as well as for the demands of kids and cares.

In prayer, God can gently remind us of what His real priorities are—and ours.

For instance, it's God's expressed desire that *every man be a priest and prophet in his own house!* He's supposed to be the leader, actually filling those two offices for his family: speaking to God on behalf of his wife and kids, and speaking to his family as God's mouthpiece. Too few men today have any idea of this responsibility. If their kids are to have any kind of spiritual leadership, they look to a minister or a teacher—or to Mom. Anywhere but to Dad, who's "too busy." I thank God for the countless mothers who *have* assumed spiritual leadership, because otherwise their kids would never have had any spiritual guidance—but God never intended woman to be the leader. From creation onward, God meant for her to be at her husband's *side*, implementing his leadership and partnering with him in the achieving of their mutual goals.

Most men ought to be horsewhipped for abdicating their responsibility. They've virtually forced their wives into priestly roles, if their family has room for God at all.

As a result, things get mixed up and out of proportion, and religion becomes "her thing."

Eventually the bill comes due. I'm thinking of a well-known singer, a friend of mine, whose wife became a regular churchgoer and managed to hold the family together when he was out drinking and messing around with other women. But then the man began to see the futility of the life he was leading and the couple came over to our house a few times to explore the idea of letting the Lord do His repair work on their marriage.

It was obvious from our conversations, though, that the wife felt superior to her spouse. She was always putting him down, reminding him of his failures, and it became obvious that she was quite skeptical about his ability to change his ways.

"I think this is just another phase he's going through," she confided to me one day. "I can't help but believe that he'll eventually run off again and leave me alone with the kids."

I tried to convince her that his yearning for God might well be genuine, but she wouldn't really listen. She had a big chip on her shoulder and was almost *daring* the man to succeed in his spiritual quest. He was whipped and defenseless, rarely refuting his wife's opinion of him—and last I heard, they're still having a terrific struggle.

Another friend, a well-known comedian who has had some problems with drinking and emotional disturbances, also has strong spiritual leanings, but again, his wife has been standing in his way. This fellow and I have had many conversations about God and prayer, and I've had the strong impression that he really wants to attend the Bible studies we conduct in our home. But his wife won't hear of it.

Her attitude seems to say, "Look, I've sweated with him through his drinking and all the other problems, and now he's fairly straight. That's good enough for me. I've got him where I want him now, and I don't want anybody rocking the boat."

This woman may be afraid for her husband to develop any freedom in his spiritual life because she likes being the anchor and would feel very insecure if he began to challenge her in this area.

In both of these situations, prayer—real soul-searching honest prayer together—could work wonders! But neither of the men knows *how.* And even if a man decides he wants to learn, it may take an exceptionally understanding and compassionate wife to help him get started.

For example, one woman I know wanted very much to spend time each day in prayer with her husband, but he had just made a commitment to Christ and he felt quite unsure of himself. For one thing, he was afraid that he would make a fool of himself in front of his wife by praying the wrong way. Also, there was a slight sense of competition—he was reluctant to admit to her that there was something he didn't know, something he might even be able to learn from her.

But this wife didn't precipitate a crisis by pushing her husband too fast. She stressed how much it helped her just to have him present as she prayed, and he agreed to sit silently with his head bowed as she talked to God. After a few sessions like this, they began to talk more about their mutual concerns before she prayed, and she would always include in her prayers comments he had made during their sharing period. Then, she got into the habit of asking him exactly what he wanted her to include in her spoken prayer: "Bob, you mentioned you were worried about that oral report you're supposed to be giving next week—want me to pray about that?" she might ask.

By being tremendously patient and following this step-by-step procedure, this wife gradually led her husband very naturally into sharing her prayer life, and finally into participating openly with her. He began to see that it didn't make much sense for him to tell her what to pray for—why not just go directly to God Himself?

I love this woman and her tender approach. That's real love in action!

Like a skilled nurse, she was able to feed and exercise her patient until *he* was able to take over, stepping into a position of leadership and responsibility in which she could relax and settle into a real partnership with him.

And what about the other benefits? Don't you think that that marriage will have a much better than average chance at surviving in this goofy world? Sexual tensions tend to dissolve; mutual respect and real interdependence increases; a sense of teamwork permeates the whole family atmosphere; doubt and suspicions and uncertainties tend to vanish.

If you have to travel a lot in the nature of your work, as I do, this can make a very significant difference. Shirley really *trusts* me when I'm on the road, just as I trust her. After all our praying together—well, let me illustrate it with this true story. I was in St. Louis, and was invited after my concert to a party in the home of some well-to-do friends. I wandered back into the kitchen to raid the icebox, and a good-looking, successful young guy followed me.

"Have you got a minute so I can ask you something?" he said.

"Sure," I replied.

"Well, a bunch of us here are Christians, and I know you are, and I've got to ask somebody about this. I figure you can sympathize and maybe help me more than anyone else here because you're an entertainer and you must have gorgeous young women around you all the time. I'm working with some beautiful girls at our office, and they're attracted to me, and yet I'm married. What do you do about it?"

I almost got the impression that he was hoping I'd say, "Well, now and then it's not so bad . . . once in a while . . . everything in moderation, you know."

But instead I said, "Look, there are four things that help me with what you're facing, so let me share them with you. I nearly lost my marriage, my relationship with my wife and my family. I nearly threw it all away. We had some rocky times, and we both knew our relationship was about shot, but now we've got it back together again. And I don't want to blow it this time—*no quick fling is worth it.* That's the first point.

"The second thing is that I've been filled with the Holy Spirit, and I have a strong sense of God's presence with me at all times. And the Bible says that when we do anything like what you're talking about, we really grieve the Holy Spirit. Man, I wouldn't risk what I've got with God now for *anything;* I'd be a fool to intentionally jeopardize my close friendship with Him.

"In the third place, Hebrews 12:1 says we're 'surrounded by a great cloud of witnesses.' There's nowhere I can go to be *alone* with some woman! There's the Holy Spirit, angels, and maybe a whole host of departed loved ones watching me! So when I go into a room or a closet or under a bed or on a bed or turn out the lights or hop into the back seat of a car, I may be away from other flesh-and-blood people—but I'm still center-stage as far as these spiritual witnesses are concerned. If you *know* that's true, won't it make a big difference in what you do?

"And finally, since I've experienced this new quickening by the Holy Spirit and I'm drawing closer to God in prayer, I now see young women as spiritual beings. When I see young stewardesses or waitresses or starlets, whether they're wealthy, privileged people or just young girls I meet somewhere, I realize now that each one is a person Jesus died for. Oh, I still notice her figure, and her beauty and her personality, and I can still sort of "get turned on"—but then a quick little scene, like in a movie, races through my mind. I see her as a little girl, innocent and trusting; I see her as a mother, trying to teach her own kids what's right; I see her as an older woman, her flesh sagging and her heart unsettled about dying; and then I see her standing face-to-face with God, desperately hoping that He'll claim her as His daughter, and I realize I'm in a position to help her—or contribute to her doom. This all happens in a flash, but it sure helps get my priorities straight. And brother, it's a *relief* not to have to play that old game anymore, to be a real friend to a lovely young girl, instead of a predator."

Well, my answer in the kitchen had turned into a quasi-lecture, but the young businessman was still listening, so I told him a story about an encounter I'd had recently with a young stewardesses. This girl was spending a lot of time beside my seat on the plane and was coming on kind of strong. Then she asked, "How old are you?" When I told her I was forty-four, her jaw dropped, and then I asked, "How old are you?" and she replied, "Twenty-one."

"Yeah, my daughter Debby's your age," I said, and I could see that put a new light on our conversation.

But then she said, "Well, the *captain's* your age." And I could tell by the way she said "captain" that there might be something between them.

So then I pulled out a couple of pictures of my grandkids that I always carry and I asked her about any younger sisters or brothers she had. As she started thinking about her home and family, everything took on a different perspective. We *both* began to see her as a young girl instead of a femme fatale, the airline's answer to the Happy Hooker. We had a good warm visit as people, not like two animals in heat, and I felt the Lord enter the conversation and put His hand on her. I haven't seen her since, but I can feel good about our meeting that day—instead of guilty.

Now, it's a real world and I'm just as human as the next guy. I know from experience that if Shirley and I didn't spend a lot of time praying together, I could get real fuzzy about where my responsibilities lie. As sure as you and I are communicating right now, Shirley and I would've divorced a long time ago if God hadn't entered and healed our marriage, through our prayer life.

And what about your kids? Are you ready to be their spiritual leader? They've only got one daddy, you know, and they're looking to you to show them the way. So is the Lord!

We started having family devotionals when our girls were quite small, using little Bible storybooks and gradually working up to the Psalms and the Living Bible. As you might expect in our family, we also always sang at least one song, and we'd try to let one of the girls suggest it and lead it. Each of our daughters learned to pray spontaneously by leading the prayers during these family devotionals, and I'm sure it was their conversations with God that were carrying me through my own spiritually dry period in the 1960s, when I had drifted into the Hollywood drinking and party scene, far from the moorings of my faith. During that time, I was just going through the motions in those family prayer times, and my girls and Shirley were the ones who were really in touch with God.

Still, I was at least assuming the *position* of priest in our home, and it made a difference. My girls prayed for their daddy—and God heard them! Shirley prayed for her husband, and the Lord let me paint myself into a corner. He protected me from disgrace and from financial ruin, though the dangers and the pressure got so intense that I finally dropped to my knees and recommitted my life to Him. After a period of some spiritual rehabilitation, I was able to give my family the one thing they needed most from me in all the world—a husband and father who was *trying* to be what God wanted him to be. And through all the mistakes I've made since then, Shirley and my daughters have at least known that I was trying to be their priest and prophet.

I've spent a lot of time trying to help friends establish their relationships with God and I've discovered that those who had an interested, concerned, supportive *dad*—one who disciplined and participated with his children—find it easier to conceive of a God who has those same qualities. By the same token, it's hard for a person to believe God is loving and concerned if his own father was harsh, unforgiving and dictatorial. Or if he was unconcerned and overly permissive.

With all my imperfections and mistakes, I've had the wonderful experience of having each of my kids tell me, at one time or another, what my youngest daughter Laury recently wrote to me. She thanked me for helping her believe God was a loving Father—because *I* had been a loving father and pointed her to Him.

One of the richest rewards that can come to any man is for his children to say, "You helped me to understand God."

Since our girls were always at different age levels, and had different bedtimes, I would sort of make the rounds at night. First, I'd go to talk and pray with Laury because, as the youngest, she was in bed first. Then I'd head for the room shared by Lindy and Debby; and finally, I'd spend some time with our oldest, Cherry. That was three goodnight prayers just with the children, and Shirley and I would end the day with prayers by ourselves.

One reason I think it's important for parents to be willing to spend separate times in prayer with each of their kids at different age levels is that each child faces different problems and may not be as free about sharing deeply with a younger or older sibling. For example, Debby entered her teenage years at a time when the drug problem was getting very bad in Beverly Hills. Many kids were experimenting with pills and pot, and she was confronted head-on by the involvement of some of her close friends in the drug scene. It would have been so easy for her to succumb to peer pressure, but I believe it was primarily our family prayers and her own personal relationship with God that kept her from participating herself. In fact, she came to us one day and said, "My best friend is really messed up with drugs—could we pray for her?" And we did get on our knees and pray immediately for this girl. The story has a happy ending, by the way, not only for Debby but also for her friend: within a few days the girl came to Debby in tears and said, "I'm really loused up. Can you help me?"

Shirley and I didn't have to say a word. Debby took it from there, knowing that God had answered our prayers and was working actively with her to help her friend! How can you measure the impact and the value of an experience like that on the life of your child?

Long ago, I had to accept the sad truth that there was no way to protect my kids as much as I would like to. There was *no such thing as isolation;* but there was *insulation.*

By introducing your children in a gradual way to the many channels through which God can communicate with them, you provide them with a solid footing for grappling with all the problems of life. You can't be with your kids all the time—and it's impossible to isolate them from all the pitfalls and temptations the world has to offer. But you can help *insulate* them from within by showing them how to build a personal relationship with the Lord through prayer. When they've developed a firm faith, you can relax in the knowledge you've done all that's humanly possible to prepare them for life, and now it's up to God.

Oh, I know that a lot of people think we're hopelessly square, "old hat," behind the times, quaint and old-fashioned and maybe a little funny. But when I look at the way my daughters have matured and blossomed into radiant young womanhood, the way they've entered marriage with a full knowledge of what that commitment means and all the inner resources to make it work—I wouldn't trade places with any man on this Earth.

Debby's married now, and very proud to be Mrs. Gabriel Ferrer. You can ask my daughters, sometime, if they regret the choices made as young girls, heading toward marriage. I think you can guess their answers.

It's not easy for a dad today, and it's not easy for a family. We're absolutely riddled with what I call "world-think," a whole mind-set that is increasingly alien to what God wants to accomplish in the world, and in individual lives. Much of society has actually degenerated to the philosophical credo "If it feels good, do it!" I really wonder how far we are from the kind of environment that turned Sodom and Gomorrah into doomed cultures. The Bible has a lot to say about what the world will be like in the very last days, the windup of human history—and it can't be far different from what Hollywood and TV pour into our living rooms all the time now.

Do you want to just drift along with the tide? Do you want your marriage and family to be stacked up with all the other depressing statistics? I can't believe that you do. The only alternative is for each father and mother to assume their respective roles and responsibilities and to declare, "As for me and my house, we will serve the Lord."

You'll have to determine that you and your family are going to be different; that you're not going to do what "everybody else" does, just because they do it, right or wrong. Society won't help much, TV and newspapers and movies won't help at all, and even lots of churches offer little in the way of guidance. No, it will have to be an individual decision, a quality decision and commitment, on *your* part—and, oh yes, a little help from God.

After all, this marriage and family thing was *His* idea. He *means* for it to work, and will see that it does, if you'll let Him. He designed the family as a school of prayer; and prayer learned at home will work *anywhere*, under any circumstances!

13 The Prayer Prescription

Fatima. Lourdes.

Oral Roberts. Kathryn Kuhlman. "Be healed!"

"I can see! I can see!" "Throw away your crutches, in the name of Jesus!" "Rise up and walk!" "The Lord has healed me; it's a miracle!"

FAITH HEALER SUED: CHILD DIES.

We're about to deal with a very controversial topic. Whole libraries have been written about miraculous healing—and this is just one chapter of one book. Naturally we can't exhaust the subject, but we must deal with it, because we're talking about prayers that win. And success in any field, the accomplishing of the mightiest goals, *everything* else is hollow and empty without physical health.

Many a millionaire and powerful political leader has been willing to swap it all for the health of a stevadore. Chains of gymnasiums and health spas, giant vitamin

173

companies, health food stores and best-selling books on diet and exercise, whole new industries springing up around the obsession for health and fitness and personal appearance—all attest to a universal craving to be well, as long as possible.

Can prayer win health?

I believe it can, or I wouldn't bring up this subject.

First of all, God *created* man to be healthy and whole. He hasn't changed His mind. In fact, He never intended that we should die at all—but we loused that plan up pretty thoroughly. Lots of passages in the Bible indicate God's expressed will that we should be healthy and prosperous and blessed all our lives. "May God Himself, the God of peace, sanctify you through and through. May your whole *spirit, soul and body be kept blameless (perfect)* at the coming of Our Lord Jesus Christ. The one who calls you is faithful and He will do it." (First Thessalonians 5:23, 4) Paul spoke this, but by the inspiration of God—so it reflects God's will for us.

In the same way, the beloved disciple John wrote, "Dear friend, I pray that you may enjoy good health and that all may go well with you, even as your soul is getting along well." (Third John:2) Interesting that he connected physical health with the soul's prosperity, isn't it?

That's no accident. When God made His great promises, His magnificent covenant with Abraham in Genesis 17, He tied the blessings to Abraham's faith and obedience. Later, He expanded the whole concept in His promises to Israel in Deuteronomy 28, offering every conceivable blessing to those who obeyed his law—and then pronouncing the most fearful curses, *including every disease and disability known to man,* on those who disregarded and disbelieved His promises.

Now don't jump to conclusions; I'm not saying, nor does the Bible, that every physical ailment is a result of a person's sin. But it is a fact that *all man's ills are the result of man's fallen state.* They did not originate with God, nor is it His will that we be afflicted.

But since man, as a race, has collectively rebelled against God, He offers health and healing to individual believers. The psalmist David knew it: "O Lord my God, I called to You for help—and you healed me." (Psalm 30)

Again, this famous and comforting quote from Psalm 91:

He who dwells in the shelter of the Most High will rest
    in the shadow of the Almighty.
I will say of the Lord, "He is my refuge and my fortress,
My God, in whom I trust."
Surely he will save you from the fowler's snare
And from the deadly pestilence.

Like the Psalms, the Proverbs are filled with similar promises: "Do not be wise in your own eyes; fear the Lord and shun evil. *This will bring health to your body and nourishment to your bones.*" (Proverbs 3)

Again Solomon advises in Proverbs 4, "My son, pay attention to what I say; listen closely to my words. Do not let them out of your sight, keep them within your heart; *for they are life to those who find them and health to a man's whole body.*"

You may feel I'm giving you too much Scripture, but I feel it's important that you understand that it's God's will for you to be healthy!

"Okay, okay. But I didn't know that, and I'm already sick. What do I do about it now?" Well, I'll have to give you a few more Scriptures, so you'll know how to pray according to God's will.

"Jesus went through all the towns and villages, teaching in their Synagogues, preaching the good news of the Kingdom and *healing every disease and sickness.*" (Matthew 9) And after his resurrection, just before He ascended to the throne of his Father to be the direct channel for our prayers, He told his disciples, "And these signs will accompany those who believe: in My name they will drive out demons; they will speak in new tongues; they will pick up snakes with their hands; and when they drink deadly poison, it will not hurt them at all; *and they will place their hands on sick people, and they will get well.*" (Mark 16)

There are lots of other Scriptures, but these illustrate God's willingness and eagerness to heal every disease, in response to (a) faithful prayer and (b) in the name of Jesus. These are absolute prerequisites. Some people get well without one or another of these ingredients, but there is certainly no Scriptural guarantee.

A leper approached Jesus in Matthew 8, just after He had completed his Sermon on the Mount. You'll agree that leprosy is a pretty tough disease to handle, right? The leper said, "Lord if you will, you can make me clean." And Jesus responded by stretching out His hand and touching him and saying, "I will; be clean." The leprosy was cured immediately because the man had asked in faith and according to God's will.

Jesus was even more explicit about the need for faith during the course of other such miraculous healings. He told the woman who was cured of a long-standing hemorrhage after touching his garment, "your faith has made you well." (Matthew 9:22) A blind man who asked to be healed while sitting on a roadside near Jericho was told, "Receive your sight; your faith has made you well." (Luke 18:41) And the servant of a centurion who was stationed in Capernaum was cured of paralysis when the centurion told Jesus, "Lord, I am not worthy to have you come under my roof; but only say the word, and my servant will be healed." Jesus responded, "Truly, I say to you, not even in Israel have I found such faith," and the servant was healed right then. (Matthew 8:5-13)

But even if these miracles of healing occurred when Jesus was on Earth, what proof do we have that they weren't limited to Biblical times? For one thing, Jesus promised in John 14:12, "Truly, truly, I say to you, *he who believes in Me* will also do the works that I do; and greater works than these will he do, because I go to the Father." Greater works than these . . . those are challenging words. But history has proved their truth.

Let's take a look at John Wesley, who wasn't known primarily for his healing ministry but still saw some miraculous answers to prayer in his travels around England. In fact, the reports of supernatural events resulting from his ministry were so striking that jealous church leaders like William Warburton, Lord Bishop of Gloucester, criticized him openly for being a fanatic.

Warburton's attacks became so vicious and inaccurate that Wesley felt compelled to respond in a letter to the bishop written in 1763. Far from playing down the reports of mircaulous healings, Wesley vigorously reaffirmed that God was acting supernaturally in the eighteenth century much as He had done in Biblical times:

—"In the evening I called upon Ann Calcut. She had been speechless for some time. But almost as soon as we began to pray God restored her speech. . . ."

—"I visited several ill of the spotted fever, which had been extremely mortal. But God had said, 'Hitherto shalt thou come.' (Job 38:11) I believe there was not one with whom we visited who didn't recover."

—"Mr. Meyrich . . . had been speechless and senseless for some time. A few of us joined in prayer. Before we had done, his sense and his speech returned. Others may account for this by natural causes. I believe this is the power of God."

Wesley's conclusion in his letter to the bishop sums up the impact of these healing miracles better than I can: "But what does all this prove? Not that I claim any gift above other men; but only that I believe God now hears and answers prayer, even beyond the ordinary course of nature. Otherwise the clerk was in the right, who (in order to prevent the *fanaticism* of his rector) told him, 'Sir, you should not pray for fair weather yet, for the moon does not change till Saturday.'"

But remember—Jesus said "He who believes in Me" would experience these things, and that doesn't just mean religious leaders, does it? No, lots of folks in ordinary contemporary life are discovering that *their* names are written at the end of those scriptures, too!

Avion Brooks, an official at Delta Airlines in New York City, found that her active, athletic life was likely to be severely restricted by a chronic knee problem until she discovered the full power of healing prayer. But she can tell her story much better than I can, so here it is in her own words:

The doctor's report came as a shock. I would have to go back in the hospital again for tests on my knees.

Seven years before, I had had an operation on my right knee for a degenerative bone disease for which there is no cure. At the time, the doctor had come just short of removing my kneecap altogether.

"You're a twenty-four-year-old woman, and I can't make you a clinical invalid for the rest of your life," he had said.

After the operation, I was grateful that my kneecap was still intact and that as a result I would not be stiff-legged. But my recovery was slow and painful. It took six months before I could walk up and down stairs without taking one step at a time, and a year before I could run a short distance.

Although I had made progress, I was constantly burdened by the knowledge that my knee wasn't healed, and that someday I might have to face a recurrence and another trip to the hospital. The doctor had warned, "You can do anything you want, Avion, but if you should fall on your knees, the bones might crack."

I made a vow to myself that I would never go back to the hospital and never put myself through the painful recovery. So with the doctor's warning ringing in my ears, I held myself back from the physical activities I loved. I had been on the women's swim team in college. I loved to run, play tennis, and go bike riding. But I was afraid to enjoy them. I became a prisoner of my own fears.

When my friends would call and say, "Let's play tennis," I'd answer quickly, "I can't." My knees became an excuse for not exerting myself physically. As a result, I started gaining weight. Before I knew it, I was twenty pounds overweight, and I looked and acted like a lump.

During the next few years, I didn't think much about the changes that had taken place in me. Although my knee hurt every now and then, I figured I could live with a few aches and pains. As for my job, I had an exciting career with an airline and loved the people I worked with.

Then without warning two years ago, I collapsed in pain on the couch in the adult Bible study at church. I felt as though a hot poker had just pierced my knee, and my face contorted in agony. Just as quickly as it had come, the pain passed, and I tossed it off as a freak occurrence. But as the weeks went by, the acute pains became more frequent. At work I would bend over to pick up a paper clip off the floor, and a wrenching pain would hit my knee. Or I'd be out shopping with a friend and be racked with pain as I stepped off a curb onto the street.

The doctor put it to me bluntly. "It's gotten worse, Avion. You've got to go back in the hospital for an exploratory exam so that I can see how bad it is."

I panicked. The thought of another operation—of going back into the hospital and living through the same horrible ordeal of a long rehabilitation, and possibly having my kneecap removed—was more than I could bear.

Here I was, just turned thirty, and my life seemed to be falling apart. I had just broken up with my boyfriend after a five-year romance. We had talked about marriage, but it just didn't work out. And now this operation loomed before me.

Just thinking about it made me break into tears. At work, friends would say sympathetically, "Sorry to hear that you need another operation." And I would start crying.

Along with my tears, I also started praying. I asked, "God, help me with this problem, take it from me." Two years before I had accepted Christ in a wonderful, Spirit-filled experience. I had begun to read the Bible every day, and I had wanted to understand more about what God wanted from my life.

Now, faced with the operation, I turned to Him in desperation. All day long—a hundred times a day, it seemed—I prayed that He would take the problem away. Although I believe that God had the power to heal, I couldn't bring myself to ask specifically for a healing. So I simply said, "God, help me with this problem." Yet no matter how often I prayed, I would go through the day frightened at the operation, and weeping at the mere mention of it.

But God was beginning to answer me in small, though significant ways. One Sunday after church, I stood before the mirror in my living room and just looked at myself. And I didn't like what I saw. I was overweight, out of shape and unattractive.

Suddenly it hit me. Up until then, I had read the Bible—but it had been an intellectual exercise. I wasn't applying it to myself, in that I didn't regard myself literally as the temple of God.

I looked myself straight in the eye and said, "You know, you're thirty years old, and God is giving you the chance to start over again."

I now realized that in order to let other people love me, I had to love myself first. So I began a program of exercise and dieting to make the "temple" fit for God and for myself.

God also spoke to me through my doctor. When I called him to schedule a time to go into the hospital, he asked how I was feeling. "Fine," I said. "The pain isn't as bad." Surprisingly, he told me to wait. "If your knees don't hurt too much right now, maybe there's no need to put you through this. Call me in a month."

I was ecstatic. In high spirits, I flew off to Tampa to visit relatives, thankful for even a momentary respite from the hospital. I've always felt very close to God in planes, and on this trip I felt especially close. The plane was empty, and I had an overwhelming sense that I was alone with God up there in the clouds. As I had been doing for weeks, I started praying that God would help me. But then something compelled me to go further and ask *why* I still had the problem.

I put it to God directly: "I can't understand it, God," I prayed. "If I keep giving You the problem, why do I still have it?" He didn't take long to answer. His voice was as clear as if He had been a fellow passenger sitting next to me: "You keep giving it to Me, and then you keep pulling it back!"

Tears streamed down my face. For the first time, I realized I had not been willing to let go of the anguish I felt, of the worry, and of the pain. I felt a tremendous sense of relief. This time I knew I had given the problem to God for good and would never take it back. As I walked off the plane in Tampa, I knew I didn't have to worry. No matter what happened—healing, or no healing—it was in God's hands.

And I could also see that God had been trying to break through to me during the past few weeks. The day I faced myself in the mirror and embarked on an exercise program—that was all part of God's plan for me.

When I returned from Tampa and called the doctor, he postponed the hospitalization again. I knew that God was at work. By now, four months had passed since that first depressing visit to the doctor. I was filled with anticipation as I went with friends to Jesus '76—an ingathering of Christians from all over the country who wanted to share their Christian experiences. There, I had a chance to hear Pat Robertson, host of the 700 Club, and to witness firsthand some healings taking place around me as he spoke and prayed in Jesus' name.

I still held back from asking God specifically to heal me. Somehow, I didn't yet have the courage to believe that God could and would heal me as He had healed others. But then I heard the testimony of a former convict and dope addict, and his words seemed to be directed straight at me.

"If you have the faith, you can claim things in the name of Christ and they will come to pass," he said. He told how he was on the brink of death after being stabbed by a hit man. His mother prayed over him, claimed him on faith in Jesus' name, and his life was spared. A few years later, his inner life was healed as he accepted Christ and became a new man.

"Could I claim such a healing for myself?" I asked God. Again I listened for an answer as I had on the plane to Tampa. And the message was just as clear. "If you accept it on faith, you have it."

I believed, and I was healed. Like the centurion whose belief in Christ caused his son to be healed, and like the woman whose issue of blood ceased when, on faith, she touched the hem of Jesus' robe, I had taken God at His Word.

My knees felt like they were brand new. I felt a tremendous urge to run. Up until then, I couldn't run a block or run upstairs without getting a throbbing pain in my knees. But those pains were forgotten as I sprinted a mile back to the campsite.

Instead of throbbing with pain, I bubbled over with thanks for the health that surged through my knees. As I shared my experience with my friends, we jumped up and down for joy.

All the way back to New York, I praised God for my healed knees. I was still thanking Him as I walked down the steps of the plane, but then I felt a small twinge of pain in my knee again. I froze in my steps.

"God, You healed me—what is this?" I demanded. Again God spoke to me: "You are healed because you believe. But you can't stop where you are."

Right then I knew what I had to do. I had only lost ten pounds since I had started exercising. And I knew I still had a long way to go spiritually as well. But I also had God's assurance that if I moved toward these goals, someday I would be totally cured.

My doctor verified the dramatic change in my condition. "I can't put you in the hospital," he said, when I went for an exam after Jesus '76. "I can't pick up any trace of the disease. Just keep on doing what you're doing."

What I've been doing is praising God. I praise God for where I was, where I am now, and what I have to do. I can have fun on the tennis court now and I know what it's like to be able to run. I'm a lot luckier than a person who has had perfect health all her life. I'm beginning to understand my own body—my strengths and weaknesses. And I've gained a greater sense of dependence on God than ever before.

I can't say that my knees have been cured to the point where I feel absolutely no pain at all. Every now and then I do get a twinge. But in a way I almost look forward to it because I regard those twinges as God's barometer. His barometer lets me know what I still have to do—make my body a temple of God, and become more Christlike in my personal relations. Most of all, His barometer is a reminder of how much my life depends on Him.

And for the first time, I have come to understand the meaning of Philippians 4:13: "I have the strength to face all conditions by the power that Christ gives me."

To me, the greatest thing is not the healing of my knees, but the deepening of my faith. And that truly is a miracle from God.

I find this story very moving, and very constructive; I've included the whole detailed account so that you can share the ups and downs of a miracle—which is actually a growth process. Often, when these stories are told, most of the details are left out, and a skeptical or even hopeful listener gets the impression that it always occurs like some kind of magic trick. Certainly the Lord *can* change things dramatically in the twinkling of an eye—but if He always did that, He'd have to figure out some other way to teach us what He wants us to learn, about Him and about ourselves. Avion has told you that *a healing did occur—a supernatural intervention that defies explanation—and she knows Whom to thank for it.*

In *A Miracle a Day Keeps the Devil Away,* I've written about thirty-one miracles that have happened to me and members of my family. Some of these are very dramatic medical miracles, a couple of them instantaneous. But since I've written about those already, let me tell you what happened to one of the seven children of Arthur DeMoss and his wife, Nancy, a number of years ago. Their son Paul, who was then two and a half, developed a bad cold, but things swiftly went from bad to worse. The boy started behaving very erratically, with periods of screaming, attempting to pull out his hair, and banging his head against his headboard. They kept in touch with their doctor by phone, but didn't think things had deteriorated so far yet that hospitalization was needed.

Shortly after these symptoms had begun. Art was involved in a telephone conversation with Bill Bright, head of Campus Crusade for Christ International, and Nancy decided to look in on Paul to be sure he was all right. What she encountered when she entered his room threw her into a state of total alarm.

"He was acting like an animal, writhing on the floor, carrying on pathetically," she recalled. "I managed to hold him long enough to take his temperature, and I found it had gone up to 110! I was panicked. I remember bundling him in my arms and rushing in to Art while he was still on the phone and saying, 'Tell Bill how this child is acting! He's got a fever of 110!'"

The three of them immediately decided to pray, with Art and Nancy in their living room and Bill Bright on the phone miles away. "As I recall, Art and Bill were praying specifically for what Art was witnessing about Paul's condition," Nancy said. "They asked God to help him settle down and to bring the fever down. Then I think Art asked for wisdom for the doctors that would be treating him. As I held little Paul during this prayer, I didn't feel any great surge of faith—I was probably going on Art's and Bill's prayers, I guess. It was kind of a helpless feeling. But as the two men proceeded with their prayer, *I could see little Paul settle down right before my eyes.* It was a beautiful experience. Where he had been struggling before, now it was almost as though someone had given him a sedative. Within an hour, his temperature was almost down to normal."

Nancy says that she knows now that if the high temperature had continued through the night, Paul would have suffered permanent brain damage. As it was, the medical people held out little hope for his full recovery.

"I've heard about you and your husband and I know you're probably praying," one neurologist told Nancy. "But I just hope you're not praying for your boy to make it, because if he does, he's going to be a vegetable." Paul, it seems, had a serious case of encephalitis, and there was a strong likelihood he had already suffered brain damage.

But there was great power in the prayer of the two DeMosses and Bill Bright. Remember how we discussed the multiplication of prayer power when two or more people agree together according to God's Word? Well, those three and many others kept right on praying—through the six months of treatment—and I'm thrilled to report to you that young Paul DeMoss *has now recovered completely and is one of the stellar athletes and students at the Stony Brook School on Long Island!*

But remember, too, what we discussed about the spiritual war we're engaged in. The physical attack on Paul was not the end of the DeMoss' problems. Any family as large as theirs, with the deep spiritual commitment and power influence they have, is bound to have more than one battle. And so it's been! The dramatic healing of their young son helped prepare Nancy for an even more drastic physical threat to her own life. She'd begun to have some difficulty with her hearing, and since the problem was getting steadily worse, she sought the advice of medical specialists. The diagnosis was devastating: They said she had a massive brain tumor that had wrapped itself around the auditory nerve and if she didn't have immediate surgery, she wouldn't be alive in six months.

"To be perfectly honest, I wanted to go to heaven," Nancy said, describing her first response to this news. "What was always lurking in my mind was the possibility of paralysis, but then I realized that it wasn't my prerogative to choose the conditions under which I would live. So I asked the Lord's forgiveness for trying to take matters into my own hands and I said I didn't want to go home to heaven unless He wanted me there. I told Him I'd be happy in whatever shape I was in, but *I wanted Him to give me complete joy*—not just acceptance, but joy."

As the DeMosses' friends around the world heard about her impending surgery, Nancy got cards and telegrams every day that assured her many prayers were being offered on her behalf. And her sense of God's presence kept her spirits up even as they wheeled her into the operating room. As a matter of fact, she actually sat up on the stretcher as her doctors gathered around her to prepare her for the operation, and asked if she might talk with them! Try to imagine the impact of what she did, on those good professionals who were about to perform an extremely delicate brain operation on her!

"I came to know Christ in a personal way some years ago," Nancy told them, "and I want you to know He is not only in control of my soul, but of my life as well. Whatever happens in the next few hours is in His hands, and I want you to know He's going to use you because He's really in control in this operating room."

As it happened, it was more important than anyone realized for God to be in control during Nancy's surgery.

When the doctors opened her up and took a look at the tumor, they didn't expect her to leave the hospital. Or if she did survive, they didn't think she would walk or talk again because so many nerves had been damaged by the tumor.

The primary surgeon, though, had an interesting experience as he proceeded with the operation: He said later, "I had the distinct impression that I was not the surgeon in the room today." Those who had been praying so hard for Nancy's recovery would have known exactly what he meant.

When Nancy awoke several hours later, she was in bad shape, and it almost seemed as though the doctors' dire predictions were going to come true after all. She spoke very gutturally and had no facial movements at all in her eyes and mouth and no control over her right arm. But the prayer she had offered before the operation—that she would be filled with joy—was answered as soon as she opened her eyes. "Art told me that in the twenty-some years of our marriage he's never seen such joy coming from me. I didn't know at that point whether I'd be paralyzed forever, *yet I was totally joyous*—it was a beautiful experience."

This infusion of joy wasn't the only answered prayer, either. Gradually, Nancy improved until now her healing process has been so complete that it would be impossible to tell that she's had an operation. "It was miraculous," she says. "I feel that I've had just as much a divine healing as if God had reached down into my head and taken that tumor out. But there's one additional thing: I had been a singer all my life and performed frequently. But after the surgery, I had no singing voice and it's never come back. When the doctors first told me I wouldn't be able to sing, the first thought that went through my head was, 'Now I can't do anything well.' There was some sense of accomplishment in singing well. And there was also some pride involved. I had always told myself I was singing for the Lord, but occasionally there were times when I really wondered what was in first place—the music or the Lord. The music kind of held too close a second place, I think. Soon I got a new appreciation of my salvation that was really mind-boggling. I saw *everything* was dependent on Him. This new, fresh understanding of what He had done for me made me realize He had acted for my own good, and I can honestly say now I'm not bitter at all about the fact that I can't sing anymore."

Nancy DeMoss will be singing enthusiastically and well, throughout eternity! She's just taking "a breather."

Healing accompanied by deepening spirituality—without any question, that's what miraculous prayer is all about. I don't believe God's primarily interested in "patching up" bodies that are destined for a grave anyway. He's certainly not trying to "put on a show" or do tricks for our amusement, or even our delight. Jesus raised His old friend Lazarus from the dead—but Lazarus eventually died again anyway. So what was the point? Jesus tells us Himself: When Lazarus' sister sent word to Jesus, "Lord, the one you love is sick," Jesus answered, "This sickness will not end in death. No, it is for God's glory, *so that God's Son may be glorified through it.*" (John 11)

That makes sense, doesn't it? Since we are all under a sentence of physical death anyway, and since a far better, more perfect eternal life is waiting for those of us who have committed our destinies into the hands of the Living God—why bother patching up leaky inner tubes? When the eternal steel-belted radial is on its way? Two reasons: God really cares about our welfare *now*, and He wants to draw us closer to His saving Son.

And so He uses us to minister to each other, whether we are doctors or not. I've already pointed you to

Scriptures in Mark 16 and James 5, in which the Lord promises physical healing—through the laying on of the hands of other believers! He intends for us to need each other, and to operate in Jesus' name! He won't always permit "maverick spirituality"—He demands an inter-relationship, a mutual dependence on each other and on Jesus for our continued perfect health.

And so, my family and I have seen multitudes of miracles, when we've joined in prayer for others. Cancers have disappeared, broken limbs have been healed instantly, hearing and eyesight have been restored, asthma and other chronic ailments have vanished, practically everything but resurrection from the dead. And a couple of our close friends have even witnessed that!

Through all of these things, two patterns have surfaced. Though there have been some occasions of instantaneous healing, an unexplainable miraculous reversal of the normal physical process, most of the healings we've been part of have been gradual or in stages, like a Polaroid picture developing. The situations have kept lots of believers praying for a long time, and have really multiplied the joy through larger circles when the cure was pronounced. And secondly, the physical healings have *always* encouraged and resulted from growing commitment to God and His way of life.

And that's an extremely important point. It's very hard for most of us to understand or appreciate, but *the real reason for our existence is to glorify and please the Living God!* That's true! If our lives don't accomplish that, then they're just an exercise in futility, a temporary blip on the scan of creation, an inconsequential fungus or chemical accident, like all the atheists say. But if our lives are pointed toward God, and if we're eager to please Him, blessing just naturally flows toward us, and shining physical health is often one of the benefits!

However—there are still mysteries. I wish I could tell

you that I and my family and friends have come up with a foolproof method, an approach to sickness and physical calamity that works one hundred percent of the time, but I can't. We see God's plan and principles too imperfectly, and there are times when healing takes a different and higher form than the one we'd prescribe.

I'm thinking about Eric White. Eric was a beautiful seven-year-old boy when I met him with his parents, Bill and Judy. Bill was a local minister in the State of Washington, who promoted a Christian concert with my family and me. Our families became long-distance friends, and we were stunned when Bill called us one day to tell us Eric had leukemia. We prayed together on the phone, and then they brought Eric down to our home, and I was shocked by the physical change in him. His body was swollen and his hair was virtually gone, but there was an inner light that seemed to shine through in his eyes. He was actually happy, so full of love and determination to get well! In fact, he *knew* he was going to get well—that was evident as we laid our hands on him, anointed him with oil after the Biblical tradition (James 5:14) and prayed for him.

And he *did* recover for a while, but then the leukemia came back and he had to go into the hospital. This time, Dennis Bennett, the Episcopal priest and author, prayed with him and once again—even though the doctors said he'd never leave the hospital—he had a remission and was able to resume a normal life. Whole communities of people, in several States now, were rejoicing at the news that young Eric was back in school and running around like a normal healthy boy.

But a few months later he was back in the hospital. Things were really serious this time, because Eric had slipped into a coma and we were afraid we had lost him for good. The pessimistic doctors predicted he wouldn't come out of it at all, and if he did, they said, he would be

191

a mental vegetable. But we all prayed and Eric returned to consciousness, as happy and loving and full of God's spirit as ever. Our main hope was that he would get completely well, but he just kept saying, "All I want is to be with Jesus." Whether in this world or the next, he had come to desire a relationship with God above all else, and his deep faith, so mature for one so young, absolutely pierced the heart of each person who met him. And there were hundreds of them—friends, and strangers, doctors and ministers, old and young.

Eric did expect to get well and he had all the little-boy ambitions about what he would do when he grew up. And he especially wanted to please his parents, who wanted so much for him to recover. But the main priority in his life seemed to be Jesus Christ. Whatever Jesus wanted was what he wanted. We prayed for him and enjoyed him for three years.

And then he died.

I couldn't understand it at first. In a way, God almost seemed to have let us down, to have ignored, at the end, all our heartfelt supplications to Him for this little boy. But as I thought about Eric's short life here on earth, I came to a different conclusion.

Bill and I intend to write a book about Eric, to tell his story in detail, and to share with others some deep and glorious truths God taught us through Eric's short, radiant life. There's too much to go into here, but one of the central facts we must each confront, starkly and with fear and trembling, is that the God of Heaven and Earth allowed His own Son, a supremely innocent young man, to die a horrible death Himself, slaughtered like an innocent lamb nearly two thousand years ago so that we imperfect human beings, who *deserve* to die, might live. There's no escaping that reality, for any of us, and the death of young innocents like Eric today, though they can't save us as Jesus' death did, do force all of us to look again at the terrible decadence of man in his fallen state, and the consequences of life—and death—in separation from our Creator.

Bill White preached the sermon at little Eric's funeral. For the multitudes that attended, it was a moment etched in time and bathed in tears. Ten other ministers helped with the service, and hundreds wept as they thought of Eric and the deep impact he had on their own lives and priorities. I met Eric when he was seven—and he died at ten—but I've met few people in any walk of life who've had more of a lasting influence on me than Eric.

I told Bill and Judy later, "You know, there won't be a whole lot of people who, after living seventy or more years, can stand before the Lord and say, *'I've brought You a hundred others.'* Yet little Eric, who only lived ten years, will be able to say that."

Can you accept it when I tell you that little Eric White is a prayer winner? True, his winning battles seemed to set the stage for a crushing defeat in the war, but remember—Eric had a higher priority than being physically well! Since he'd been able to talk, as a very little boy, he'd seemed attracted to Heaven, in love with Jesus and his Heavenly Father. Like Jesus in the agony of Gethsemane's garden, he wanted to please God more than he wanted to live. And so God used the desire of little Eric's heart, his ultimate prayer, in a way that few of us can understand or appreciate.

But think a moment: try to imagine Eric now, try to fathom in the most finite degree the reception when he flew to the heart of his Eternal Father. Eric's story isn't finished; his dad and I plan to see to that, with God's help. But far better than that, his life has only begun!

There are victories, and they can be sweet. We all want victories. But there is *winning*, in its ultimate and highest sense—and that's really what this book is about.

14   The Root of All Riches

Would you like to be a millionaire? It's fine with God!

Lots of people *don't*, of course. They realize, quite sensibly, that a lot of money brings with it increased responsibilities, risks and complexities, and they don't want to be bothered. They're quite content to live moderately, have all their essential needs met, and keep their pleasures simple and inexpensive. They also like to fill out the short form when income tax time comes around. My hat's really off to them.

I guess I've been a millionaire, at least on paper, for twenty years now. There have been lots of advantages, of course, but I've often wondered if my family would have been happier, qualitatively, if we'd had less money and more time. For most people, lots of money means lots of work, before, during and after. It's been wisely said, "You don't own things, brother; they own you!"

Ernest Hemingway wrote, near the end of his life, "The more mature a man becomes, the fewer possessions he wants or needs."

194

Still, it's a very materialistic world today, and there's a great emphasis on money and possessions. Lots of people *want* more money—and that's okay with God. He'll help you get it, in fact—*if* you're willing to accept the responsibilities that come with riches, and if you're willing to let Him lead you in the acquiring of your wealth. He talks a lot about getting and staying rich in the Bible, especially in the Book of Proverbs. It's a great "how-to" book on material prosperity. And though He declares that "the *love* of money is the root of all evil," material wealth in itself is *not* evil, and He Himself is the ultimate source of it!

But that's the main point. It's a matter of priorities. *He* has to be first, your ultimate source, or riches can wreck your life. If money is your God, you're a walking dead man. And no loving father wants that for his son. In his very first recorded sermon, the matchless Sermon on the Mount, Jesus acknowledged that God knows our needs for all material things, but added, "the gentiles seek all these things; and your Heavenly Father knows you need them all. But seek *first* His Kingdom and His righteousness, *and all these things should be yours as well.*" (Matthew 6)

So what's the key to having material abundance? Exactly what we're doing right now—finding out what God's will is, and then praying it into action.

David, "a man after God's own heart," knew the formula.

> Blessed is the man who fears the Lord,
> Who finds great delight in His commands.
> His children will be mighty in the land;
> Each generation of the upright will be blessed.
> *Wealth and riches* are in his house,
> And his righteousness endures forever.
> (Psalm 112)

Knowing God's will, he confidently prayed:

> . . . may our garners be full, providing all manner
> of store;
> may our sheep bring forth thousands and ten
> thousands in our fields;
> may our cattle be heavy with young, suffering no
> mischance or failure in bearing;
> may there be no cry of distress in our streets!
> Happy the people to whom such blessings fall!
> Happy the people whose God is the Lord!
> (Psalm 144:13-15)

And God *answered* David's prayer beyond his dreams! He made David wealthy and powerful and respected throughout the known world, and blessed his son Solomon even more. As a young man succeeding his father to the throne of Israel, Solomon asked God not for money or power, but for wisdom. He wanted to be a good king, and this delighted God so much that He made Solomon the wisest man that ever lived—as well as the richest and most powerful! These guys knew how to pray!

But even after you know that God wants you to prosper, it's not quite as easy as just asking and then opening up a bank account. There are conditions and qualifications, and I'm learning more about them all the time. In fact, God uses our desire for money to teach us a *lot* of things. For instance, the writer James cautions that we won't receive what we ask for if we "ask wrongly, to spend it on your passions." (James 4:3) God knows what's going on inside your head; He understands your motives even better than you do. So be sure when you pray about your finances that you've put Him and not your "passions," as James puts it, in first place.

Want to know a real shortcut to riches? *"Pray and*

give; give and pray." Though this is a Biblical principle, I learned it the hard way. When my show business career first started to do well, I would give 20 to 30 percent of my gross income to the Lord in various ways, and my managers would say, "You'll never have anything—you give it all away!"

But the truth was that the money just kept rolling in— hit songs, television appearances, movies—I couldn't give my money away fast enough! But then I gradually drifted away from God, and my giving went down bit by bit until I dropped way below my tithe of 10 percent, which is the bare minimum God asks of us. (See Malachi 3:10; Luke 11:42) Soon I was looking exclusively for donation schemes that offered large tax benefits, and I'd end up getting almost as much back from the IRS as I gave. In effect, I wasn't really *giving* anything away at all!

Then things started to go wrong, not only with my inner spirituality and my family relationships, but with my personal finances as well. I made a series of bad business commitments, and for a while it seemed certain that I'd lose everything and have to go into bankruptcy. For one thing, I had invested in the Oakland Oaks basketball team—a colossal financial washout, an economic "black hole"—and one day I received a terse letter from the Bank of America, demanding immediate payment of 1.3 million, in cash! I had already paid out seven hundred thousand dollars, and I just didn't have the cash on hand and had no idea where I could get it. Only a miracle could save me from disaster.

But fortunately, as I detailed in *A New Song,* I'd begun to learn about miracles. I'd recently turned my whole life over to the Lord, been filled with His Holy Spirit, and my education in God's deep "abundant life" principles had begun. As a result, I was surrounded by some strong Christians who *knew* God was going to rescue me from this impending disaster. My friends Harald Bredesen, George Otis and Harold McNaughton took me aside at a Bible study at George's home one evening, just after I'd received the Bank of America's demand. They assured me that God wasn't going to let me go bankrupt and then they laid their hands on me and prayed, "Lord, God, we ask You for a massive and immediate miracle."

A tremendous sense of assurance swept over me, and I began thanking God and rejoicing that He was going to pull me through this disaster. I expressed this sense of assurance to other friends and business associates, including my attorneys, and of course they all thought I was crazy. But within two days—just in the nick of time, like some sort of divine cavalry charge—*a man none of us knew flew in from Washington, D.C., and bought the Oakland Oaks for nearly two million dollars.* Oh, he had his own reasons, but it was a miracle regardless. If he'd waited one more day, he could have bought the whole mess for half a million dollars—and I'd have been bankrupt. The timing was too exquisite for it to have been a coincidence. There's a lot more to this story, but those are the highlights.

However—my Holy Spirit "crash course" in finance had just begun. I had a lot more learning to do, and a few more knotholes to be drug through. In addition to this basketball team deal, I had also become a general partner in a large and successful real estate company. After a dozen years of unbroken and accelerating success, with major land developments in the United States and Australia, the severe recession of 1970 threw us into a financial tailspin, and we found ourselves desperately struggling to reorganize and save the company under the Chapter Twelve provision of the Bankruptcy Law. Because of my legal status in the firm, I was threatened with the company's entire thirty million dollars in liabilities—and that was at least twenty-seven million dollars more than I could have scraped together under any circumstances!

It was "SOS" time again—and for the second time in my life, God spoke to me over the radio!

Driving along one day, feeling utterly helpless in this latest financial catastrophe, I idly tuned across the radio dial and "happened" to hear a minister talking about giving—and he said, "Every year in the United States and Canada, without fail, the insurance companies record about a ten percent loss in crops. You can count on it—a ten percent loss due to what they call 'acts of God,' like droughts, floods, blights and other natural disasters. One way or another, *God demands His tithe!*"

The preacher went on to say that, according to an extensive poll, farmers who tithed regularly fared a whole lot better, even when the weather was hostile, than those people who don't give to God. And I thought, "Man, you're talking directly to me!"

Now I don't know about this preacher's statistics, but I do know that God was using him to put a finger on a major problem in my finances. I had recommitted my life to Christ and I was learning things I had never known before about the power of prayer. But I was still giving piddling sums to God's work and to other human beings who needed money far more than I did. So I knew right then exactly what I had to do.

I called my accountant in and I said, "John, we've got to get more serious about my giving. I want to give a tenth out of every dollar I earn."

"Wait a minute," he protested. "You're talking about ten percent of your gross! That's something like twenty percent of your net income!"

"Okay, but I give about ten percent to the agency that books me, and I give ten percent to my manager," I replied. "I'd better give ten percent to God if I expect Him to show me the way out of my financial problems."

"You can't afford to," he stated flatly.

"I can't afford *not* to!"

So I started tithing again, and it felt good. As each dollar came in, John faithfully set aside at least a dime of it, and we started The Pat Boone Foundation. This was just to be a channel through which I would give to God and to various individuals and organizations that were engaged in the advancement of His Kingdom, and at first there weren't a whole lot of dimes coming in. But now I was praying with new fervor and expectancy, and my income began to pick up noticeably. I urged my partners in the real estate company to pray, too, and a number of them committed themselves to do just that. We knew that, without God's intervention, there was absolutely no way out of our dilema. Not only did they pray, they rolled up their sleeves and worked like crazy! I went about my business, singing and making records and doing television and personal appearances—and praying. At the end of the first year of this new giving program, I met with John, and he was shaking his head.

"I may be your accountant, but I don't know how this has happened," he said. "You've paid all your expenses, you've reduced your debts, you've paid all your taxes and you've even started a pension fund—all this in spite of the fact that you've been giving ten percent off the top!"

"No, it's *because* I've been giving ten percent off the top," I corrected him.

As I said, I've had to learn the hard way that you can't outgive God. It seems to me that He's built some sort of generosity principle into the universe which assures us that if we combine prayer and generous giving, He'll return to us far more than we've laid out. Or as Paul in Second Corinthians 9:6 says, "The point is this: he who sows sparingly will also reap sparingly, and he who sows bountifully will also reap bountifully."

So I find that I'm in a giving contest with God, based

on Jesus' promise: "Give, and it will be given to you. A good measure, pressed down, shaken together and running over, will be *poured into your lap.* For with the measure you use, it will be measured to you." (Luke 6)

And it works! The more I give, the more it comes pouring back; then I step up my giving, but so does God. This book is about winning—but this is one contest I'm glad to lose!

Still, no matter how much you give and pray, financial crises still crop up. I think God uses these difficulties to give us a chance to learn more about trusting Him and also to broaden the scope of our supernatural dialogue.

One good illustration of this process involved Art DeMoss again, who probably knew as much about risk-taking entrepreneurial financing as anybody in this country. He had just founded the National Liberty Corporation, and the company had started off "in high gear," to use Art's words. "We pushed it very hard in terms of growth, and we were skating right on the edge, on thin ice. I remember running four-page ads in the *Reader's Digest* which were costing one hundred and fifty thousand dollars each—and at the time that cost exceeded the total assets of the company. So they *had* to work!"

The growth of the company had been so fast, however, that DeMoss started running into serious financial trouble in 1963. His accountant told him one day in going over the books, "I'm afraid there's just no way you're going to make it, no way you're going to be able to come out of this."

Art recalled, "We had overexpanded and owed money. There's always a problem in a new business of coordinating or synchronizing your cash flow, with the right balance of income and outgo. We had borrowed a lot of money to 'leverage' the company and make it expand faster, and we owed about one million dollars, which was a lot of money for me at that time." The money was due in a few months, at the end of the year, and Art had no idea how he would come up with it.

As if these debts weren't enough, he also learned that another company was negotiating to buy a group of insurance policies that contributed to a large part of his business. These policies were owned by a Midwestern insurance organization for which DeMoss had, in effect, been acting as agent. If this deal went through, it would cause Art to lose control of a significant portion of his entrepreneurial empire.

He realized that the only possible course of action he could take to save his business was to try to buy those insurance policies himself, but that would have cost *another* one million dollars. Where could he possibly get this money if he was already facing about one million dollars in bills he couldn't pay?

Art decided to set up an appointment with the president of the buying company—despite the seeming futility of trying to purchase the policies. But if you know how to pray, the "impossible" becomes merely difficult. Jesus said—ironically, in the context of discussing the difficulty with which rich people would enter Heaven—"what is impossible with me is possible with God." (Luke 18) Art DeMoss knew this, and he knew his God, and he spent a great deal of time asking for wisdom one night just before he left on this fateful business trip. "I didn't pray for money," he recalled. "I just prayed for guidance." And immediately a complex financial idea formed in his mind—an idea which, if both sides agreed, could make more money for all the parties than would have been possible under the original plan.

In essence, Art's idea—or perhaps it would be more accurate to say the idea that God gave to Art—involved, first of all, asking the other company to reinsure, or guarantee payment, on all of the National Liberty's policies in return for a percentage of the business. The plan also called for the other company to *lend Art the money* to buy the policies that were up for sale and also pay off all his outstanding debts. In other words, Art wanted the president of the other company to give him a total of two million dollars to cover both his debts and the purchase of the policies!

As Harald Bredesen says, "Make it easy on yourself and hard on God," and Art wasn't afraid to do that. And though the plan promised tremendous benefits for Art and his company, it also stood to be more profitable for the other company, if they agreed to go along with him. But Art's idea was highly sophisticated and complex, and there was no guarantee that the other president would agree to it.

At his meeting with the president of the other company, Art presented the reinsurance aspect of the deal first, and the man agreed, saying, "Go ahead and buy it and we'll reinsure!"

But then came the cruncher: "The catch is that we don't have the money to buy, and I would need to borrow that from you," Art said.

To Art's delight and amazement, the president agreed, and National Liberty received the two million dollars it needed both to avoid the serious financial difficulties and also to buy those insurance policies.

"This kind of thing has helped to give me a great equanimity and confidence in a God who answers prayer," Art said later. "And even though I don't get easily upset or overly elated about things, I guess I'd have to say I was obviously delighted at the way this thing turned out. I pretty much expected the Lord to work things out, but I wasn't expecting that two million dollars—that was truly remarkable. The president took me over to the bank where he was on the board of directors, and between his company and the bank I got a loan that required me to repay at the rate of one hundred thousand dollars a month. And the Lord allowed us to make every payment right on the button! It worked out beautifully. I don't believe the Lord always gives us exactly what we're looking for, but I do believe in Romans 8:28, that whether or not we get our prayers answered just as we want, God always works things out for the greatest good for those who love Him."

There are at least two dozen stories I'd like to tell you.

I'd like to tell you how my own daughters, almost from their earliest years, learned that they could give to the Lord out of their allowances, and He'd multiply it back to them! I'd love you to know the story about the woman with three kids who wrote me she was living with them in a car, with few dollars left to survive—and what happened after I wrote her back that she should take half of what she had left and give it to someone else, in Jesus' name! I'd love to discuss the Rockefeller fortune, and the way the Rockefeller net worth at least doubles each year, though the established family policy, starting with old John D., has been to *give away* half of the family fortune in each generation!

But we're almost out of space and time. One last question; I think I hear someone asking, "But wait a minute! Didn't Jesus say something about a real Christian selling everything he has and giving it to the poor?"

Yes, He did. But He said it to one specific man, recorded in the tenth chapter of Mark. This was a young fellow who was attracted to Jesus and wanted to be one of His disciples, part of His "road company." Jesus, with His unique ability to read our hearts, saw that the young man's *top priority* was his family wealth; that he might follow Jesus and enjoy the company of the other disciples, but he would still be relying on his "nest egg" to see him through if things really got rough. He wouldn't really be trusting God with everything.

"Yes, but He still told him to sell it all and give it away, didn't he?"

That's right—but keep reading in that chapter. In just the next few verses, He reiterated that it was extremely difficult for a rich man to get to Heaven, but that God would make it possible. And then, when Peter spoke up that he and the other disciples had left *everything* to follow Jesus, He makes this astonishing promise: "I tell you the truth, no one who has left home or brothers or sisters or mother or father or children or fields, for Me and the Gospel, will fail *to receive a hundred times as much in this present age* (homes, brothers, sisters, mothers, children, and fields—and with them, persecutions) and in the age to come, eternal life."

So how could that rich young man have lost? If he'd done what Jesus said—sell it all and give it away—somehow, he'd have come back from his traveling with Jesus to find that his family's net worth had increased a hundred times over!

God is a giver! He *loves* to give and to bless and to multiply—but He's waiting for us to give Him *something*, so he can multiply it back to us! It's just like planting a seed and then expecting a harvest.

But notice that little phrase in Mark 10, right in the middle of the hundredfold promise, "and with them, persecutions." As we said in the beginning of this chapter, money brings responsibility and complexity and pressure—and even dangers. One of the greatest dangers is the spiritual one, the strong chance that the money will assume top priority, eventually coming to own *you* rather than the reverse.

But it's still "okay" with God; if you think you're man enough, pray to be rich.

Remember the formula: *pray and give—give and pray.*

15 How to Mix Prayer and Politics

Can religion and politics mix? Most people will say they can't—or shouldn't.

I feel the opposite.

Oh, I firmly believe we should keep politics out of the church, and separate the government (state) from the church—but I want to get as much of the church into the *state* as possible!

Now, hold on—I'm not a complete political heretic. I don't mean I believe that a giant church organization should be pulling the strings in our government—God forbid! But when I say "church," I'm using the word in the Biblical sense: the church is people. And I want to see as many God-fearing, Bible-believing, power-praying men and women active in every level of our governmental processes as we can possibly find.

At the height of the whole Watergate mess, some of the press asked Senator Barry Goldwater if future Watergates could be avoided. Goldwater thought just a minute and shot back, "Sure; quit printing dollar bills!" Then, after the press chuckled, he added thoughtfully, "Or let *men* suddenly become moral and ethical and honest."

And I think he's right. But how do men become ethical and moral and honest in this loused-up, compromising, and self-seeking world?

You've guessed it.

I'm sure you remember the Watergate trauma as I do; the agitation, the almost daily revelations, the arguing and accusations and hounding investigation, while a whole nation began to feel guilty and outraged. At the height of all that, I was doing some speaking before large groups, mainly Jesus rallies, around the country. I knew that Bible-believing people were wondering how they should feel about President Nixon—what, if anything, they should say or do.

Many times I told them, "Pray for him!" And I reminded them of Paul's *command* in First Timothy 2:1: "I urge, then, first of all, that requests, *prayers*, intercession and thanksgiving be made for everyone—for kings and all those in authority, that we may live peaceful and quiet lives in all godliness and holiness."

I reminded the audiences that this admonition was directed toward *all* in authority, and that we didn't have to make judgments about whether our leaders were right or wrong, that regardless of anything else, we were supposed to *pray* for them—so that God could work in their lives and bless *us* through them! And, inevitably, I felt the wave of relief sweep over the people as they realized they didn't have to be judge and jury—they were to commit Richard Nixon into the hands of God, and pray that God would overrule in His life, for all our sakes.

And He did.

During the last few months of his tortured Presidency,

I tried to phone Richard Nixon at the White House. We were friendly acquaintances, and he knew that I had actively campaigned for him through several election campaigns, the losers and the winners. I called regarding an upcoming National Day of Fasting and Prayer, which the Senate had proclaimed in the form of a resolution, and which it was hoped Nixon would proclaim as President. I had an additional idea which I felt would be very beneficial to Richard Nixon personally in his political fight for life—but when I conveyed the idea to the White House secretary, she connected me to his aide for "religious affairs."

Knowing the President was under extreme pressure from all sides, I decided to convey the idea to this aide, in the hope that he would understand it and relay it to the President. The idea was simply this: President Nixon should not only proclaim this date as a National Day of Fasting and Prayer, but for the first time in American history, actually *voice* a prayer via television and radio, becoming the first President to actually lead the nation in prayer. I knew that many would writhe at the idea, but Biblically and realistically the President is supposed to be the spiritual leader of the nation, its ruler and guide. I further suggested that if President Nixon led such a prayer, he could confess his own mistakes as well as the nation's, and ask God to forgive us all. In so doing, he would be making a public "confession" of his own error—but in the context of a prayer for the national good—and I felt the impact of this unprecedented event would be so tremendous that he would actually receive political benefit while he and the nation benefited spiritually. It was a perfect way to say, "Folks, I've been wrong and I acknowledge it; I hope you and the Lord will forgive me. Now let's move on."

I based my astounding proposal on several verses from the Book of Proverbs:

"When there is moral rot within a nation, its government topples easily; but with honest, sensible leaders there is stability." (Proverbs 28:2 Living Bible)

"A man who remains stiff-necked after many rebukes will suddenly be destroyed—without remedy. When the righteous thrive, the people rejoice; when the wicked rule, the people groan." (Proverbs 29: 1 and 2 NIV)

"If a ruler listens to lies, all his officials become wicked." (Proverbs 29:12 NIV)

"A man who refuses to admit his mistakes can never be successful. *But if he confesses and forsakes them, he gets another chance.*" (Proverbs 28:13 LB)

The aide was polite, and recommended that I write out a sample of the kind of prayer Nixon ought to lead and send it to them. I did, and that was the end of that. I don't know if the aide ever passed my suggestion along to the President, but needless to say, the plan wound up in File 13. Quite soon after that, Mr. Nixon was too busy resigning to mess with impractical "religious" ideas. I still think it would have been a fantastic, bold stroke of political and spiritual leadership.

Later, I came across Proverbs 29:26, "Many seek an audience with a ruler, but it is from the Lord that man gets justice."

And then, as Gerald Ford assumed the Presidency from the fallen Richard Nixon, I moved back three verses:

> A man's pride brings him low,
> But a man of lowly spirit gains honor.

What's the point of all this? The point is that *prayer, the right kind of prayer, in accordance with God's revealed will, would most likely have saved the Presidency!* It would also have meant increased health, wealth and happiness for Richard Nixon and his nation. There is a distinct and unavoidable link between prayer and national well-being and prosperity. Over and over, the Bible makes this clear: "The good influence of godly citizens causes a city to prosper, but the moral decay of the wicked drives it downhill." (Proverbs 11)

Then, time after time, the New Testament teaches us that godly citizens, praying believers, *can shape the course of history*, in partnership with the overruling God: "Let every person be subject to the governing authorities. For there is no authority except from God, and those that exist have been instituted by God." (Romans 13:1)

You might even say that God sees to it that we get the kind of government we deserve! Or need, perhaps. But the people who take God's Word seriously, and pray for their leaders and the "state of the nation," can shape their government's policies and affect its current standard of living and its destiny!

"Strong words," you say. And they are—but they're not mine. God says it Himself: "If my people will humble themselves and pray, and search for Me, and turn from their wicked ways, I will hear them from Heaven and forgive their sins *and heal their land*." (Second Chronicles 7:14)

If "my people" will pray! God's not depending on the whole population of any nation—but He has issued a directive to those who consider themselves His people, His sons and daughters. And He promises that if His "kids" will do their part, He'll look after their national affairs! Isn't that incredible?

Following this Biblical line of reasoning, Charles Colson, who had extensive experience in both the good and the bad side of politics as former President Nixon's special counsel, says, "I think we're commanded to pray for those in authority so that they can be instruments of the divine will. Government is the instrument used in a fallen world to preserve order—and it can be an instrument of justice or of evil. Of course I don't mean that all governments serve as a divine instrument because some may be so imperfect in certain policies that it's the duty of the Christian to resist. That's what Peter did when the Sanhedrin commanded him and the apostles not to preach the Gospel. He answered, 'We must obey God rather than men,' and was sentenced to a beating, but they continued to preach." (Acts 5:27-42)

In Colson's opinion, one current example of this principle of obeying the law of God rather than of man would be the issue of abortion. "If I were a judge today, and the law of the land said abortion has to be given as a matter of right, I couldn't prescribe abortion. I do not believe it's consistent with God's covenant. I'd have to say, 'That may be the law and someone will have to enforce it, but it won't be me!'"

Colson says that the key thing about praying for our governmental leaders is "to ask that they be brought in conformity with God's judgment," rather than simply asking that God bless them in their work. In other words, we should pray that the actions of our politicians serve God's will, rather than that as an afterthought, some divine imprimatur be stamped on everything they do.

But just how specific should you get in praying for your rulers? Colson believes we should pray that "those in authority will be led by the Spirit so that God can use them and they can be open to His leading. That's a lot different from praying for Republicans over Democrats."

And having been "behind the scenes" at the White House during one of its most turbulent periods, Chuck adds his conviction that it's important for the leaders *themselves* to pray.

"I would hope that the politicians themselves would pray the *true* prayer of King Solomon. Solomon was a weak young kid, and, he thought, not adequate to the task of ruling Israel. But he prayed to God, 'Give thy servant therefore an understanding mind to govern thy people, that I may discern between good and evil; for who is able to govern this thy great people?' He didn't pray that he would be successful or powerful or rich, but just that he could have the wisdom to know right from wrong and judge the people wisely. The essence of his prayer was that he wanted the ability to do justice to his people.

"Because he didn't pray for a long life or personal success, God was pleased, and He said, 'Behold, I give you a wise and discerning mind, so that none like you has been before you and none like you shall arise after you.' (First Kings 3:7-17)

"This prayer is sometimes misused by politicians because they simply ask, 'Give me the wisdom of Solomon'—and they forget that the wisdom he asked for was the *wisdom to be just to his people,* not the wisdom to become a great and successful world leader."

But can earnest, Bible-reading and God-fearing, praying people be on opposite sides of the same issue? Sure they can! We're human and limited in our understandings, and that's one of the reasons we need so desperately to pray! None of us have all the answers, but God does. And if we all pray for the national good, for our leaders, and for God's will to be done in sensitive and vital issues, it'll get done. Where even the most sincere people make their mistake is in saying, with all good intentions, "*My* will be done"!

This happened to me during the last Presidential campaign. I knew that Georgia's Jimmy Carter was a praying Christian—but Gerald Ford was a praying Michigander, and already President. I campaigned actively for Ford, and my activities took me to Atlanta, Georgia. I'd been asked by the Georgia Republicans to speak at a big

212

fund-raising rally there, and so I went. I really got wound up, and I'm afraid my enthusiasm for campaigning got the better of my good judgment and I made some tasteless political jibes at Ford's opponent, Georgia's Jimmy Carter. I didn't think much more about the episode until I met President Carter's sister Ruth after the election. She told me, "On election night, as the returns were coming in and it looked like he was going to win, Jimmy said the thing that had hurt him worst in the campaign was what you said about him in Atlanta. He was upset that you had come to his home state and campaigned against him, even though you're supposed to be his (Christian) brother."

I felt like a weasel. It really hadn't occurred to me that Jimmy Carter himself would know I'd said those things; but until that moment, if I had thought about it, I would have assumed that he would have taken them as part of the political game. But he was right, completely right, to be offended by these sort of "dog eat dog" remarks from a fellow Christian. So I sat down and wrote him a letter apologizing *not* for campaigning against him, but for making those rather rude jokes. I said I knew he was my brother and I hadn't taken that enough into consideration. I had been engaging in what I thought was political game, but I said I thought I was wrong and "would like to ask you, as my brother, to forgive me."

I gave Ruth a copy of this letter to give him, and she said normally she wouldn't do that, but under these circumstances, she would. Not long afterward, I got a note back from the President saying, "Received your letter . . . appreciated it . . . no apology necessary. Warm wishes," and it was signed, "Your brother, Jimmy."

I've since met him and apologized face to face, and President Carter was even more gracious in letting me off the hook. It's ironic (more an evidence of my inconsistency and partiality as a human being) that I asked people to pray for Richard Nixon—and poked fun at Jimmy Carter. But I'll learn.

Listen, that's a tough job! Any elected office is. I've been approached more than once to run for office myself, and after weighing the responsibilities and sacrifices involved, I decided I wouldn't touch it with a ten-foot pole, unless God demanded it of me! Especially today, politics seems a "no win" proposition—unless there's lots of prayer involved, rising from the populace *and* their elected leaders together.

I had a very revealing conversation once with Ronald Reagan, while he was Governor of California. He'd been in office only for a couple of years of his first term, and during our conversation, he began to muse, "I wonder if you can really hold on to your ideals and beliefs and still be successful in politics."

He'd been facing some particularly tough pressures and demands, and people were saying to him, "You can be a big help to us and the party if you pull this string and compromise that principle." Reagan was determined not to do it, not to "sell out"—but it was getting tough. He told me he was praying more frequently, and more fervently. Then he gave me an example of the way God was answering his prayers.

The issue of abortion had surfaced in full force in California, and he had been praying for wisdom about what position he should take. Both pro and antiabortion advocates were pressing him to declare where he stood, and he was trying to sort through his own beliefs and feelings.

Finally, after wrestling with this issue in prayer for a long time, he decided that he could support abortion in situations involving rape and where the mother's life was threatened. But he certainly couldn't endorse the procedure as an alternate method of birth control, and he

214

was also opposed to it *even in cases where there was a possibility that the child might be deformed*. He made a public statement to this effect and was still feeling unsettled when his legal assistant, Herb Ellingwood, came into the office carrying a painting.

"I thought you'd like to have this, in light of your decision," Herb said. A dynamic believer himself, Herb had been praying hard for Reagan during this period too, by the way.

The Governor looked at the canvas and saw that it hadn't been done all that expertly, and then asked, "Why would I be interested in this?"

"Because it was painted by a woman who was born with no arms or legs," Herb replied. "She had to paint this with a brush in her mouth *because she was born deformed*."

The Governor told me he looked again at the painting, and this time got goosebumps. So did I, as he told me the story.

"I think the Lord was giving you a little pat on the back," I told him.

Friend, there wouldn't be a United States of America, this minute, if it weren't for praying people! Our first president, the Continental Congress, the framers of the Constitution—all these men, though they had many personal flaws, believed in God and the power of prayer. Because they acted on this belief, and because God actively intervened in answer to their prayers, America became the strongest nation in the history of the world! Prayer has always been an integral part of our nation's development. It was a belief in the potential power of prayer in politics that prompted these words to be included in the first prayer offered in Congress: "Be Thou present, O God of Wisdom, and direct the councils of this honourable assembly; enable them to settle things on the best and surest foundation."

It was a similar conviction that caused Abraham Lincoln to set aside April 30, 1863, "as a day of national humiliation, fasting, and prayer." In a proclamation for this observance, Lincoln said, "We have been preserved these many years in peace and prosperity; we have grown in number, wealth, and power as no other nation has ever grown. *But we have forgotten God!*

"We have forgotten the gracious hand which preserved us in peace and multiplied and enriched and strengthened us, and we have vainly imagined, in the deceitfulness of our hearts, that all these blessings were produced by some superior wisdom and virtue of our own.

"Intoxicated with unbroken success, we have become too self-sufficient to feel the necessity of redeeming and preserving grace, too proud to pray to the God who made us. It behooves us, then, to *humble ourselves before the offended Power, to confess our national sins, and to pray for clemency and forgiveness.*"

What if Richard Nixon had led this kind of prayer?

Would somebody have shot him, too? I doubt it—but even with his tragic and needless death, Lincoln occupies a position in our history and in our national heart second to none. With all the gut-wrenching decisions he had to make, and with a colossal sense of his own inadequacies, Lincoln still recognized that the Presidency brought with it a responsibility for spiritual leadership, as well as political. Our greatest presidents and political leaders have been praying men, unashamed to call out to God publicly.

But we seem to have "outgrown" that; a timid Supreme Court, afraid that they might encroach on the rights of a pitiful few atheists or other nonbelievers, deprived the majority of *its right* to pray openly in schools. This is atheist Madalyn Murray O'Hare's legacy to the American people. I don't want to be around when she stands before God and tries to justify her actions—

and I wouldn't want to be one of those judges either! I wonder if they prayed before they handed down their verdict that day.

Politics *is* controversial. Political issues are often unclear and complex; how much more, then, we need to pray—openly and publicly! The *spiritual* aspects of abortion and drug legalization and divorce and open promiscuity and governmental immorality are largely ignored today—we're left with ordinary, self-centered men making decisions that affect our national destiny. What a cruel joke! I love the way Billy Graham put it: "Our problems are past human solutions; there are now only divine solutions."

We're so like the people of Israel. After God miraculously brought them out of Egyptian bondage and led them through the wilderness, providing their every need supernaturally, they balked at entering the land of Caanan. Moses had sent out twelve spies to look the new place over, and ten came back with ominous reports that the land was filled with giants. In spite of all they'd experienced, human reasoning took over and the people completely lost heart. They started planning how they could choose a new leader and head back toward Egypt. (See Numbers 13-14)

God became very angry at this faintheartedness, and He asked Moses, "How long will this people despise me? And how long will they not believe me, in spite of all the signs which I have wrought among them? I will strike them with the pestilence and disinherit them, and I will make of you a nation greater and mightier than they."

Only Moses' fervent and self-sacrificial intercession convinced God to pardon the people of Israel once more; and even then, none of those living, except Joshua and Caleb, who believed that God had the power to give them victory, were allowed to actually cross the Jordan into the Promised Land.

Interesting, isn't it? Chilling too. Of all those living when they first came to the border of Caanan, the only two who were permitted to eventually enter *were the two who believed God and practiced prayer power.* Even Moses lost patience, disobeyed God and was denied entrance. And a whole nation perished in the wilderness, through their unbelief. Their children went in, though, and the challenges they faced in the New Land really taught them how to pray!

I think we're facing the greatest challenges of our national life. And God cares! He cares about our government, He cares about our elected leaders, He cares about our economy, He cares about our liberties and opportunities, about equality and justice for all. These were *His* ideas, after all, and not our own.

Our way of life *is* expendable. Freedom and democracy are *not* guaranteed. They're not automatic. We started out as "one nation under God"—and now we're largely a fragmented, Godless, sensual and materialistic society. The only answer for us, politically and socially, is a growing army of people who know how to pray—and to vote and work and live in accordance with their own prayers.

And we could use a lot more leaders like Senator Mark Hatfield, who says, "I can't lose an election. My opponent may get more votes, but I still win because my commitment is to God's will. It's obvious to me that if an opponent gets more votes, God has some other place for me."

16 Can You Talk Your Way Into the Winner's Circle?

"Okay, guys, before we go out on the field, let's pray.

Dear God, please help us to win today. Make us a better team and help each of us to do his very best. You know we need this victory, Lord, to stay in contention for the title, so we're asking You to help us mop up the field with the other team. We don't just want to win, Lord—we want to pulverize 'em. We want to crush 'em! We want to annihilate the bums! We want to embarrass 'em so bad, they'll wish they'd never taken up the game. Thank You God! Amen.

Okay, team! Let's go out there and smash 'em!"

How does that prayer affect you? Does it make you uneasy, perhaps rub you the wrong way? Does it fit in with all the other concepts of prayer that we've discussed? Does a person, or a team, or a nation have the right to pray for its own success at the expense of others?

Before you make a hasty and glib judgment—listen to a couple of David's prayers.

O my God, save me from my enemies. Protect me from those who have come to destroy me. Preserve me from these criminals, these murderers. They lurk in ambush for my life. Strong men are out there waiting. And not because I've done them wrong.

Don't kill them—for my people soon forget such lessons—but stagger them with your power and bring them to their knees. Bring them to the dust, O Lord our Shield. They are proud, cursing liars. Angrily destroy them. Wipe them out. (Psalm 59)

David uttered that prayer, and that's only part of it, when he was surrounded by a platoon of King Saul's soldiers sent to kill him. But listen to this one!

O God of my praise, don't stand silent and aloof while the wicked slander me and tell their lies. They have no reason to hate and fight me yet they do! I love them, but even while I am praying for them, they are trying to destroy me. They return evil for good, and hatred for love.

Show him how it feels! Let lies be told about him, and bring him to court before an unfair judge. When his case is called for judgment, let him be pronounced guilty. Count his prayers as sins.

Let his years be few and brief; let others step forward to replace him. May his children become fatherless and his wife a widow; may they be evicted from their ruins of their home. May creditors seize his entire estate and strangers take all he has earned. Let no-one be kind to him; let no-one pity his fatherless children. May they die. May his family's name be blotted out in a single generation. Punish the sins of his father and mother. Don't overlook them. Think constantly about the evil things he has done, and cut off his name from the memory of man.

For he refused all kindness to others, and persecuted those in need, and hounded broken-hearted ones to death. He loved to curse others; now you curse him. He never blessed others; now don't you bless him. Cursing is as much a part of him as his clothing, or as the water he drinks, or the rich food he eats.

Now may those curses return and cling to him like his clothing or his belt. This is the Lord's punishment upon my enemies who tell lies about me and threaten me with death.

But as for me, O Lord, deal with me as your child, as one who bears your name! Because you are so kind, O Lord, deliver me. (Part of Psalm 109)

Whew! When I read that Psalm the first time, I couldn't believe my eyes. This was in the Bible? This was a prayer, from a man "after God's own heart"? I was staggered.

That sounds like the very kind of prayer that turns so many people off, that lots of folks use as an excuse not to pray at all, and to reject God and religion entirely. I've heard many men speak disdainfully of prayers uttered by bombardiers, "Lord, direct these bombs to their targets; wipe out the enemy and help us to win this war in a hurry!"

Surely, prayers uttered against others and their welfare leave a bad taste in our mouth. In the heat of a battle or a contest, lots of things seem permissible, even desirable; but later, when the dust is settled and there's time to think quietly, many thoughts and words and tactics and motives seem completely reprehensible.

"Yeah, Boone, but these prayers are in the Bible!"

Yes, they are. But there are a couple of things to consider. One is that David's life was threatened, and not because he had done his enemies harm, or acted selfishly himself. At this stage in his life, he really was a man of God's choosing and he was doing his best to obey God and bless Israel. Psalm 59 was his anguished cry as he hid in his own home from his father-in-law King Saul's soldiers. You can read the whole account in First Samuel 19 and 20, and it's as exciting a chase, cloak-and-dagger story as a James Bond film! I don't know the circumstances surrounding Psalm 109, but obviously he was being attacked again, both physically and in his character. This is a prayer of retaliation, a fervent defensive maneuver in a life-and-death situation, and not just a tactic for some kind of personal gain.

But the second consideration, and much more pertinent, is this: *David was living in a different time, under a different covenant!* Under the law of Moses, the most advanced system of justice, religion and spiritual government the world had known until then, it was permissible to take "an eye for an eye." The Sixth Commandment ordered, "Thou shalt not commit murder"; but if murder was committed, provision was made under the law for swift and violent retribution. The law of Moses recognized man's violent nature and times, and made ample provision for it. Sexual sin, sorcery, idolatry, homosexuality, mistreatment of widows and orphans, kidnapping, even disrespect and rebellion against parents—were all to be punished by death, usually stoning! "If there is serious injury, you are to take life for life, eye for eye, tooth for tooth, hand for hand, foot for foot, burn for burn, wound for wound, bruise for bruise." (Exodus 21:23) These were rough times! Society had degenerated after the fall of Adam and the cleansing, purging flood of Noah's time, to an almost elemental level, in which there was precious little regard for human life. So God gave a law that would set His people apart, educate them and *prepare* them for a far better covenant—which would be delivered and exemplified in the second Moses, His own Son.

In his very first sermon (Matthew 5) Jesus underscored the vast differences between the covenant the Jews had known and the one He was ushering in. "You have heard that it was said, 'eye for eye and tooth for tooth.' But I tell you, do not resist an evil person. If someone strikes you on the right cheek, turn to him the other also. And if someone wants to sue and take your tunic, let him have your cloak as well. If someone forces you to go one mile, go with him two miles." He went on, "You have heard that it was said, 'love your neighbour and hate your enemy.' But I tell you: love your enemies and pray for those who persecute you, that you may be sons of your Father in Heaven."

This was a whole new deal! It worked against human nature, and seemed impossible. And it *was* impossible, without the supernatural aid of God and the actual indwelling presence of His own Spirit. It was time for human nature to be transformed, and for men to rise above the dictates of their own flesh—and to start becoming sons of God.

Both covenants were sealed in blood; the first one with the blood of animal sacrifices—and the second with the blood of Jesus Himself. He suffered the ultimate violence, to begin erasing violence from human nature. He was a victim of greed and lust and envy, so that He could begin to eradicate these destructive traits from man's character. He became a divine "blotter," desiring to soak up and drain all the filth out of God's creatures.

And He taught us a totally new way to pray.

He taught us a new way to win.

Oh, man had already witnessed some powerful prayers. When David slew Goliath, when Moses parted the Red Sea—these were dramatic answers to prayer, the likes of which the world had never seen before! And we're still talking about them! And there were even *more* astounding prayer answers; yes, even more incredible than the parting of the Red Sea! For some reason, you don't hear as much about the time when Joshua, leading the people of Israel, stood outside the city of Gideon and directed the battle against five armies of Amorites who had ganged up on little Israel, trying to drive them out of the land of Caanan. But listen to this:

On the day the Lord gave the Amorites over to Israel, Joshua said to the Lord in the presence of Israel:
"Oh sun, stand still over Gideon,
Oh moon, over the valley of Aijalon."
So the sun stood still,
And the moon stopped,
Till the nation avenged itself on its enemies,
As it is written in the Book of Jashar.

The sun stopped in the middle of the sky
and delayed going down about a full day.
There has never been a day like it before or since, a day when the Lord listened to a man.
Surely the Lord was fighting for Israel!
(Joshua 10)

Now *that's* a prayer! And that's power to win!

I don't know how that happened, and I *do know* that, scientifically, we'd have to agree that the Earth probably stood still, rather than the sun and moon, since that's the way our solar system works, but the Bible describes the way it looked to all those people then, according to the knowledge they had. Recently I read the results of a computer analysis of our calendar and recorded time—and the amazing fact that there's a *gap* of almost exactly twenty-four hours in man's recorded history that the computer can't account for! I *know* this event happened—though I can't imagine how, except for the immense power of a Creator/God who is willing even to suspend the order of nature and His own creation in answer to the prayers of His believing children!

And yet, I still say that Jesus ushered in an even more powerful kind of prayer. He's not just out to win a war, to preserve a nation or repopulate a territory. *He's out to create a whole new race,* an eternal people who are destined to live with God and to share His power and authority.

My blood stirs at the thought of all this, and my heart does race, and my imagination does soar, while I contemplate God's plan for us.

But after a while, I settle back into the world as it is, and find that I'm engaged in various kinds of contests, athletic and otherwise—and I want to know how to pray in situations like that! Or should I even pray at all about such mundane things?

The answer is yes.

We're all just learning how it's supposed to be done, and people take various approaches. Prayers to win have never been strange in athletics, or to athletes themselves, and quite often the media reports on it. *People* magazine, for example, in an interview with Jack Anthony Clark, right fielder for the San Francisco Giants, stressed how Clark "sasses the umps, threw his bat an angry mile after fanning at the plate," and made obscene gestures to hecklers in the stands before his conversion. But afterward, he proclaimed, "I'm playing ball for Christ," and began to spend more time on his knees praying than he did on his feet shouting insults. He began to attribute home runs and strike outs as well to acts of God, and while he was out on the field, *People* reported, he would pray over and over, "Jesus died on the cross for our sins, and I'm a sinner, and so, Lord, please forgive me for my sins."

That would have seemed a very strange prayer to David—but Jack Clark is living under a different covenant!

Many athletes were quick to say, though, that they pray *only* to do their best, not to win over their opponents. They may attribute their triumphs to the inner strength God gives them, but that doesn't necessarily mean their prayers are specifically directed toward victory. When Dennis Ralston was the U.S. Davis Cup captain, for example, he took the American tennis stars to Rumania for the final challenge round. Stan Smith, then the top U.S. singles player, and his cohorts would be facing Ilie Nastase and Ion Tiriac, and the best-of-five series of matches promised to be particularly tough.

For one thing, the Rumanian fans were highly partisan, and Nastase and Tiriac were known for their psychological warfare against opponents. To make matters worse, some Black September terrorist threats had resulted in the confinement of the U.S. team to their hotel—primarily because of the presence of two American Jewish players. But Stan Smith was an experienced Christian, and Ralston was moving quickly in that direction, so a time of serious prayer seemed called for before the matches began. Ralston says he prayed, "Lord, give me the strength not to lose my cool, my temper," and he and Smith asked for God's support in the matches, though he stresses, "We never prayed for victory."

Smith went on to *win* his matches despite the hostile fans and distractions of his opponents. And Ralston, in coaching the team, kept his temper—though he confesses he was prepared to slug Tiriac with a racket after the Rumanian tried what Ralston considered some unfair tactics against Tom Gorman, another American player. The Americans won 3-2, and the way God had answered the team's prayers was a major factor in moving Ralston toward a firmer commitment to Christ after he arrived back home. Who knows what would have happened if they hadn't prayed? The fact is that Dennis *knows* God stabilized that volatile situation in Rumania—and stabilized his own life for eternity as well! That's real victory!

And a similar kind of situation arose a few years later on a golf course in Tallahassee. It was the scene of the 1975 Tallahassee Open, and pro golfer Rik Massengale had just lost the lead and was feeling quite discouraged. He had been on the pro tour for several years but had never won a tournament. He had come close, to be sure, but at the last minute, he always seemed to fold up.

In addition to his golf worries, Rik was going through a spiritual crisis at the same time. He had been attending a pro golfers' Bible study and was trying to decide just where he stood in relation to God. This inner crisis came to a head that day in Tallahassee, as he turned a frustrated eye toward the next hole and recalled that his wife, Cindy, had told him what God really cared about was Rik's faith in Him.

With his thoughts and emotions churning, he bowed his head right there on the course and prayed, "Lord, I do believe in You. I can only do so much, I know. Help me find the strength to go on."

Then Rik told *Guideposts* magazine, a "surge of power and confidence" flowed through him and he recovered his lead, and went on to win his first pro tournament. He had prayed a prayer of total commitment, and as a direct result of that prayer, he won.

Massengale's prayer, of course, wasn't a straightforward prayer for victory, but rather a prayer for strength.

Are there any circumstances, though, where a direct prayer to win would be appropriate?

Tom Landry, coach of the Dallas Cowboys, gave me an interesting answer to this question. It's well known that Tom, his star quarterback Roger Staubach, and a number of others on the team are believing, practicing Christians. They're a praying bunch, the Cowboys, both collectively and individually. Tom told me, "Normally, we have chapel services prior to each game we play here in Texas Stadium. It's a voluntary type of thing about two hours before game time. Then we have a team prayer right before we go out onto the field. This consists of thirty seconds of private prayer, and then I usually close it. My basic prayer at this time is first to ask God to help us be the best we can with whatever gifts we have, and second, to ask Him to protect us from injury."

In Landry's own private prayer life, he says, "I can't imagine praying for victory just for the sake of victory, because when we play we often have good Christians on both sides. It's hard to believe that God is going to intercede in a football game when you have Roger Staubach against Terry Bradshaw or Staubach against Craig Morton. Those men are all pretty strong Christians."

But at the same time, he noted, "It's important at times that a certain player be successful because of the personal makeup of the player. It may be very important for him to perform exceptionally well for the sake of his own personal development; in those cases, I could pray that God be with him and cause him to excel. Also I could see there might be certain circumstances where it's important for Christians to have an excellent platform to witness for God. In those cases, I think it would be possible to pray to win a game. I don't remember praying to win a game myself, but I guess I might have some time. I've played a lot of football games, and it's hard to say what you really did do at one time."

Thinking back on his career as coach of the Cowboys,

Landry said, "Back in 1966 through 1968—those were tough years for us. We lost to Green Bay a couple of years in a row, and then we had two disastrous games with Cleveland in the playoffs. Everybody was so down on us that I'm sure at that time, just for the psychological advantage, for the lift it might have given, I'm sure I might have prayed at that time that we might win. But my prayer wouldn't have been for the victory as such, but for the results that could come from it. I think a team might come to the point sometimes where a victory can change their course, one way or the other. The Lord might know that a win would make all the difference.

"A win is sometimes especially important for the individual player who needs to feel more secure about himself. The spiritually mature person might be able to withstand a series of setbacks, but the less mature guy might be finished by one too many failures. His playing life may hang in the balance. In that situation, I feel it would be very appropriate to pray for him to win or have success. But this prayer to win has to result in something that benefits a human being's outlook on life, or even the entire team's outlook. That kind of prayer is quite different from praying for a victory when Pittsburgh and Dallas go head-to-head in the Super Bowl."

As an illustration of this principle, Landry referred once again to Dallas' troubles in the late 1960s. "Our team got very low during that period," he recalled. "The Green Bay Packers deserved to beat us at first, but when we reached the point where we deserved to win, we didn't. That was a tough situation—especially in 1970, when our team lost to St. Louis 38-0 in a Monday night game. By that time we had finally developed the high-quality kind of team which could go on to win a Super Bowl, but we just didn't do it. We didn't play well, and everybody was saying we couldn't win the big one. That kind of gnaws on you after a while—it makes you ineffective as a player. That was what was happening to our entire team.

"So I'm sure I prayed after that St. Louis game. We were three games behind with only four games to go, but there was a spirit that developed in that football team, and I'm sure that I prayed for it. That prayer would have been to give that team the ability to do the best they could under pressure. And all of a sudden, something moved that team. Whatever it was, I don't know, but it was uncanny the way that team recovered and played. We won seven games in a row and went all the way to the Super Bowl. We finally lost on a field goal by Baltimore in the last play of the Super Bowl. Something drastic certainly happened, but it wasn't so much what I did, except to include that team's problems as part of my prayer life."

The coach emphasized, though, that praying to win like this must focus on the needs of the individuals involved, and "not the benefits they're going to receive from victory. The important thing is what winning means from a spiritual viewpoint, what the impact will be on the guy's character or inner being, his future. Sometimes, everything depends on a special lift at a certain point, regardless of whether it's winning a football game, or getting a pat on the back, or just being loved. It's a feeling you get with some people—a sense it's important for them to be successful, not for the sake of the glory that comes with victory, but more for that personal lift that's occasionally needed."

He's a different kind of coach, isn't he? If he'd lived under the Mosaic covenant, Tom Landry would have made a great Joshua—but he didn't. He lives under a better and higher covenant, and he prays a different kind of prayer. He's making a great Tom Landry. And he's helping to make better men of the guys he coaches. That's a far better kind of winning.

There's got to be a balance in all of this, a healthy desire to achieve and to win and to accomplish our goals—but at the same time, a willingness to submit to God's will and His higher viewpoint. As we've seen, Jesus teaches time and again, "Ask what you will!" "Ask *anything* in my name!" James says, "You do not have, because you do not ask." (James 4:2) God wants us to be happy and successful and victorious, and He'll help us toward those goals in countless ways, large and small.

But Jesus also taught us to pray: "Thy Kingdom come; thy will be done, on Earth as it is in Heaven." We might call some plays, but God's coaching the game—He knows our skills and needs and can read the opposition's defenses better than we can. Not only that, He loves our opponents as much as He loves us, and is just as interested in *their* eternal destiny!

Knowing this, coach Landry has come up with this formula: he spends at least thirty minutes each morning in prayer and Bible reading and then prays off and on during the day and reads the Bible before bed at night. He also meditates on selected verses and prays "to get rid of the pain" as he's taking his two-mile run each morning. Being in this frequent attitude of prayer makes Landry quite sensitive to God's responses, and the divine answers "often come in a way that makes me feel as though I didn't do anything to bring them about. I may have worked hard and made all the right decisions, but the successful result may occur in such a way that I don't feel like I'm even a part of it. It's as though it wasn't because of the moves I made, but the result of some force outside myself. I think the Lord can work through us like this. He can use victories to further His Kingdom by putting you into positions where you know

231

your success in His work and not yours."

What can I add to that? Nothing, really—except perhaps this comforting psalm for Roger Staubach or Terry Bradshaw:

> A righteous man may have many troubles,
> But the Lord delivers him from them all;
> He protects all His bones,
> Not one of them will be broken.
> (Psalm 34)

Conclusion
Final Thoughts on Winning Big

Caesar is dead.

So are Alexander the Great and Napoleon and Attila the Hun.

Croesus and Solomon are no more; they've been joined by Howard Hughes and J. Paul Getty and H. L. Hunt.

Babe Ruth is gone, and so are Red Grange and Lou Gehrig and Rocky Marciano. Einstein and Schweitzer and Michelangelo and Da Vinci have all left the field, and though a few of their momentous achievements remain, they themselves are molding in their graves. Mao Tse-tung and Confucius and Mohammed and Buddha, though they've left deep footprints, no longer exist in this world. The greatest doers, the "largest" men and women in human history, the real giants in every field of human endeavour, have ceased to be, and their memories and their monuments become less relevant with each passing day.

Soon after the death of a famed multimillionaire,

someone asked, "How much did he leave?" The answer came sharply, *"All* of it."

So what does it all mean? It means that human victories, no matter how exciting or encompassing or dramatic, are relatively short-lived, temporary. When the dust of battle and the exertion of striving are spent, there seems to ring a hollow, echolike voice in the halls of history: "That's fine, splendid. Next?"

There must be more to life than that. And there is!

That's why I've taken the time and trouble to write this book. I want you to be a winner, in the largest and most profound and enduring sense. I want us both to pray our way into an eternal winners' circle, to savor triumphs that won't pass away, victories that matter on a never-ending scale.

Jesus *lives.*

Most of the other great leaders, in religious and other fields of endeavour, have long since crumbled to dust, and the rest are headed in the same direction. But Jesus got out of this world alive! He ascended to the right hand of God, and at this moment is supervising the advance of His Kingdom on this Earth. He didn't just reveal truth or point out beauty or indicate a direction for His followers; He's the only being in all of history who could say, "I AM THE WAY, I AM THE TRUTH, I AM LIFE. No man can come to the Father except through me."

And he rose from the dead to underscore His statement! After two thousand years, He still continues to loom as the most important figure in human history, and all the progress and all man's greatest advances, culturally and medically and politically, have been achieved through following His simple precepts. And very soon now, very soon, He'll be reentering this physical dimension with the shout of angels and a blare of heavenly trumpets, to end the game and tally the

234

score. He'll be handing out prizes to the winners—and I want you to be one of them!

I hope you don't feel that I have been devious, that I have tricked you in any way, by using your own motivations and your own earthly goals to try to sell you "some kind of religion." Believe me, I wouldn't waste my time.

God *is* interested in your goals, no matter how small or how dynamic. He *does* promise to partner with you in the accomplishing of those objectives, and I've tried to make that plain. But there's a far more important aspect to all of this: God wants to make you *His* partner in the accomplishment of *His* objectives. He wants *you* to share with Him in winning the whole ballgame!

And I know you'll find, as I have, that once you have achieved some of your most precious objectives, after some of your wildest dreams have come true, you'll be left with a sense of emptiness and disappointment. You may ask, in the words of Randy Newman's song, "Is That All There Is?" Life's just like that; half the fun is getting there, and a goal achieved is often like cotton candy. If you'll practice these prayer principles, if you'll really get into God's Word, if you'll really begin to listen for His voice and try to harmonize your specific and general goals with His revealed truth—I'm certain that you'll start to get excited about this simple fact: *changed lives* are more worthwhile, more fascinating and fulfilling, than any material triumph.

God wants you to be more than a Senator or a chairman of the board or an Olympic Gold Medalist or a Pulitzer Prize-author or a multimillionaire. He wants you to become a son or daughter of the Living God! He wants you to be a king and a priest and a Prophet, to be a people-changer and an Eternal Kingdom advancer.

Does that excite you at all? As you consider how

quickly your life is passing, and how soon it will all come to an end, doesn't your heart stir with a desire for immortality, for acceptance with the Living Lord? Wouldn't you really rather hear Him say, "Well done, good and faithful servant. Come on home, son (or daughter)" than anything else in life?

Isn't that the ultimate victory?

Not long ago, Shirley and I were invited to speak and sing at the First Annual International Prayer Breakfast of the American Family Life Insurance Company, at their convention in Honolulu. I met the three Amos brothers, who run this giant and ever-expanding company, and asked them why they were having a Prayer Breakfast. They said, "We feel it's important. We know that God has built our company, and that our hope for its future success is in His hands. A lot of our people believe the way we do, and we feel we ought to get together, at least once a year, and pray for the effectiveness of our company, and the even more important effectiveness of our lives as individuals."

I asked, "How did you come to believe all this so strongly?"

They answered, "It was our dad. He started the company, and he taught each of us. He taught us the insurance business, but more important than that, he taught us about God. This Prayer Breakfast is in his memory, and in his name."

And then they told me about his worn old Bible, which they discovered when he died. In the front of it, in his own handwriting, were key verses of Scripture that had guided his life and shaped his thinking and his policies. They were some of the very Scriptures that I've quoted to you, from Proverbs and Jesus' own words. Scriptures like:

Commit to the Lord whatever you do,
And your plans will succeed.
(Proverbs 16:3)

The Lord delights in the way of the man
Whose steps He has made firm;
Though he stumble, he will not fall,
For the Lord upholds him with His hand.
I was young and now I am old,
Yet I have never seen the righteous forsaken
Or their children begging bread.
They're always generous and lend freely;
Their children will be blessed.
(Psalm 37:23-6)

But seek *first* His Kingdom and His Righteousness,
And *all these things* will be given to you as well.
(Matthew 6:33)

The Amos boys are winners! So was Art DeMoss and so are Nancy and their kids. So is Donald Siebert and Rik Massengale and Tom Landry and all the other prayer people I've told you about in this book. So is little Eric White.

So am I.

And now, hopefully—so are you.